EAST ANGLIAN ARCHAEOLOGY

This volume is dedicated to the memory of Jennie P. Coy who was a Research Fellow in the Faunal Remains Unit at the Department of Archaeology, University of Southampton.

When I was beginning my PhD research on the faunal remains from West Stow, Jennie welcomed me into her lab and into her home. Without her help, I would not be where I am today. Rest in peace, Jennie. We miss you.

Provisioning Ipswich:
Animal Remains from the Saxon and Medieval Town

by Pam J. Crabtree

East Anglian Archaeology
Report No. 174, 2021

Archaeological Service
Suffolk County Council

EAST ANGLIAN ARCHAEOLOGY
REPORT NO.174

Published by
Archaeological Service
Suffolk County Council
Bury Resource Centre
Hollow Road
Bury St Edmunds IP32 7AY

in conjunction with
ALGAO East
www.algao.org.uk/england

Editor: Faye Minter
Managing Editor: Jenny Glazebrook

Editorial Board:
James Albone, Historic England
Abby Antrobus, Historic England
Brian Ayers, University of East Anglia
Stewart Bryant, Archaeological Consultant
Kasia Gdaniec, Historic Environment, Cambridgeshire County Council
Andrew Hutcheson, University of East Anglia
Maria Medlycott, Historic Environment, Essex County Council
Faye Minter, Historic Environment, Suffolk County Council
Zoe Outram, Historic England Science Adviser
John Percival, Historic Environment, Norfolk County Counci
Adrian Tindall, Archaeological Consultant
Jess Tipper, Historic England
Simon Wood, Historic Environment, Hertfordshire County Council

Set in Times New Roman by Jenny Glazebrook using Corel Ventura™
Printed by Henry Ling Limited, The Dorset Press

© ARCHAEOLOGICAL SERVICE, SUFFOLK COUNTY COUNCIL

ISBN 978 0 9568747 6 4

Published with the aid of funding from the New York University Center for the Humanities and Suffolk Archaeological Service.

East Anglian Archaeology was established in 1975 by the Scole Committee for Archaeology in East Anglia. The scope of the series expanded in 2002 to include all six eastern counties. Responsibility for publication rests with the editorial board in partnership with the Association of Local Government Archaeological Officers, East of England (ALGAO East).

For details of *East Anglian Archaeology*, see last page

Cover illustration
Excavation in progress at IAS 3104, Buttermarket

Contents

List of Figures v
List of Tables vi
Acknowledgements viii
Preface viii
Summary/Résumé/Zusammenfassung ix

Chapter 1. Background to the Study of the Ipswich Animal Remains
I. Introduction 1
II. Archaeological Context: Excavations at Ipswich 1
  Early Middle Saxon Ipswich (*c.* AD 600–700) 1
  Middle Saxon Ipswich (AD 700–850/880) 2
  Early Late Saxon Ipswich (*c.* AD 850/880–900) 2
  Middle Late Saxon Ipswich (*c.* AD 900–1000) 2
  Early Medieval Ipswich (*c.* AD 1000–1150) 3
III. Materials and Methods 3

Chapter 2. Animal Bones from Middle Saxon Ipswich
I. Introduction 7
II. The Archaeology of the '*Wics*' 7
III. The Composition of the Middle Saxon Faunal Assemblage from Ipswich 8
IV. Domestic Animals from Middle Saxon Ipswich 13
  Domestic Mammals 13
  Domestic Birds 21
V. Provisioning Middle Saxon Ipswich 21

Chapter 3. Animal Bones from Early Late Saxon Ipswich
I. Introduction 23
II. The Composition of the Early Late Saxon Faunal Assemblage from Ipswich 23
III. Domestic Animals from Early Late Saxon Ipswich 25
  Domestic Mammals 25
  Domestic Birds 32
IV. Provisioning Early Late Saxon Ipswich 32

Chapter 4. Animal Bones from Middle Late Saxon Ipswich
I. Introduction 33
II. The Composition of the Middle Late Saxon Faunal Assemblage from Ipswich 34
III. Domestic Animals from Middle Late Saxon Ipswich 35
  Domestic Mammals 36
  Domestic Birds 39
IV. Provisioning Middle Late Saxon Ipswich 40

Chapter 5. Animal Bones from Early Medieval Ipswich
I. Introduction 41
II. The Composition of the Early Medieval Faunal Assemblage from Ipswich 41
III. Domestic Animals from Early Medieval Ipswich 43
  Domestic Mammals 43
  Domestic Birds 47
IV. Provisioning Early Medieval Ipswich 48

Chapter 6. Conclusions and Future Directions
I. Introduction 49
II. Species Ratios 49
III. Cattle 49
IV. Pigs 50
V. Caprines 50
VI. Horses 51
VII. Dogs 51
VIII. Poultry 51
IX. Urban Provisioning at Ipswich 52
X. Future Directions 52

Appendix: faunal remains from other periods in Ipswich, and amphibian remains 54

Bibliography 56
Index, by Sue Vaughan 61

List of Figures

Figure 1.1 Map of Ipswich showing the location of the sites that were excavated as part of the Origins of Ipswich project 4

Middle Saxon
Figure 2.1 Map of eastern England and northwest Europe showing the sites discussed in this volume 6
Figure 2.2 Species ratios based on NISP for cattle, sheep/goat, pig and horse remains from Early Middle Saxon and Middle Saxon Ipswich 10
Figure 2.3 Species ratios based on NISP for the cattle, sheep/goat, pig and horse remains from Middle Saxon Ipswich 10
Figure 2.4 Species ratios based on NISP for cattle, sheep/goats and pigs from Middle Saxon Hamwic, York, Lundenwic (Opera House site), and Ipswich 11
Figure 2.5 Species ratios based on NISP for Middle Saxon Ipswich and 8th–10th-century Antwerp 13
Figure 2.6 Mandible Wear Stages for Middle Saxon cattle from Ipswich 14

Figure 2.7 Distribution of withers heights for cattle from Early Saxon West Stow and Middle Saxon Ipswich   15
Figure 2.8 Principal Components Analysis (PCA) for complete cattle metacarpals from Middle Saxon, Early Late Saxon, Late Saxon and Early Medieval Ipswich   18
Figure 2.9 Male and female cattle from Saxon and Medieval Ipswich based on PCA   18
Figure 2.10 Age profile based on dental eruption and wear for Middle Saxon pigs from Ipswich   19
Figure 2.11 Age profile based on dental eruption and wear for Middle Saxon sheep and goats from Ipswich   20
Figure 2.12 Z-scores for chicken limb bones from Middle Saxon Ipswich   21

Early Late Saxon
Figure 3.1 Species ratios for Early Late Saxon Ipswich based on NISP   24
Figure 3.2 Species ratios based on NISP Early Late Saxon Ipswich (excluding 4201)   24
Figure 3.3 Distribution of withers heights for cattle from Early Late Saxon Ipswich   27
Figure 3.4 Distribution of distal tibial breadths (Bd) for Middle Saxon and Early Late Saxon cattle from Ipswich   27
Figure 3.5 Distribution of Mandible Wear Stages for cattle from Early Late Saxon Ipswich   27
Figure 3.6 Distribution of Mandible Wear Stages for pigs from Early Late Saxon Ipswich   29
Figure 3.7 Distribution of withers heights for sheep from Middle Saxon and Early Late Saxon Ipswich   30
Figure 3.8 Distribution of Mandible Wear Stages for sheep and goats from Early Late Saxon Ipswich   30
Figure 3.9 Distribution of Mandible Wear Stages from Early Late Saxon Ipswich compared to the mandible wear data from Early Saxon West Stow   30

Middle Late Saxon
Figure 4.1 Species ratios based on NISP for the large domestic mammals from Middle Late Saxon Ipswich   34

Figure 4.2 Mandible Wear Stages for cattle from Middle Late Saxon Ipswich   36
Figure 4.3 Mandible Wear Stages for pigs from Middle Late Saxon Ipswich   36
Figure 4.4 Mandible Wear Stages for sheep and goats from Middle Late Saxon Ipswich   39

Early Medieval
Figure 5.1 Species ratios based on NISP for the large domestic mammal remains from Early Medieval Ipswich   42
Figure 5.2 Distribution of distal tibial breadths (Bd) for Middle Saxon, Early Late Saxon, Middle Late Saxon and Early Medieval cattle from Ipswich   43
Figure 5.3 Distribution of withers heights for Middle Saxon, Early Late Saxon, Middle Late Saxon and Early Medieval cattle from Ipswich   44
Figure 5.4 Distribution of Mandible Wear Stages for Early Medieval cattle from Ipswich   44
Figure 5.5 Distribution of Mandible Wear Stages for Early Medieval pigs from Ipswich   44
Figure 5.6 Distribution of Mandible Wear Stages for Early Medieval sheep and goats from Ipswich   46
Figure 5.7 Age classes based on dental eruption and wear for sheep and goats from Middle Saxon, Early Late Saxon, Middle Late Saxon and Early Medieval Ipswich   47
Figure 5.8 Z-scores calculated for the greatest lengths (GL) of chicken humeri, ulnae, femora and tibiotarsi from Early Medieval Ipswich   48

Conclusions
Figure 6.1 Species ratios for the large domestic mammals from Middle Saxon, Early Late Saxon, Middle Late Saxon and Early Medieval Ipswich   49
Figure 6.2 Age classes based on dental eruption and wear for cattle from Middle Saxon, Early Late Saxon, Middle Late Saxon and Early Medieval Ipswich   50
Figure 6.3 Lengths of the pig lower third molars from Middle Saxon, Early Late Saxon, Middle Late Saxon and Early Medieval Ipswich   51

List of Tables

Table 1.1 Chronological framework for the Ipswich excavations, based on Wade (2013)   2

Middle Saxon
Table 2.1 List of identified bird and mammal remains recovered from eleven Middle Saxon sites in Ipswich   9
Table 2.2 Species ratios based on NISP for the cattle, sheep/goat, pig and horse remains recovered from Early Middle Saxon and Middle Saxon contexts in Ipswich   10
Table 2.3 Species ratios based on NISP from Middle Saxon Ipswich compared to the species ratios from a number of contemporary sites in England and on the Continent   11
Table 2.4 Body-part distribution for pigs from Middle Saxon Ipswich and Wicken Bonhunt   12
Table 2.5 Comparison of the numbers (NISP) and proportions of cranial and main limb bone elements at Middle Saxon Ipswich and Wicken Bonhunt   12
Table 2.6 Body-part distribution for cattle, sheep/goats, pigs and horses from Middle Saxon Ipswich   14

Table 2.7	Epiphyseal fusion data for cattle from Middle Saxon Ipswich	16
Table 2.8	Osteometric data for cattle from Middle Saxon Ipswich	15
Table 2.9	Measurements taken on complete cattle metacarpi from Middle Saxon, Early Late Saxon, Middle Late Saxon and Early Medieval contexts in Ipswich	17
Table 2.10	Epiphyseal fusion data for pig limb bones from Middle Saxon Ipswich	17
Table 2.11	Osteometric data for pigs from Middle Saxon Ipswich	19
Table 2.12	Osteometric data for caprines from Middle Saxon Ipswich	19
Table 2.13	Epiphyseal fusion data for sheep from Middle Saxon Ipswich	20
Table 2.14	Withers height estimates for horses from Middle Saxon Ipswich	21
Table 2.15	Measurements taken on domestic chicken bones from Middle Saxon Ipswich	21

Early Late Saxon

Table 3.1	List of bird and mammal remains recovered from ten Early Late Saxon sites in Ipswich	
Table 3.2	Species ratios based on NISP for cattle, sheep/goats, pigs and horses from Early Late Saxon Ipswich	24
Table 3.3	Body-part distributions for cattle, sheep/goat, pig and horse bones from Early Late Saxon sites in Ipswich	26
Table 3.4	Measurements taken on cattle bones from Early Late Saxon sites in Ipswich	26
Table 3.5	Ageing data based on epiphyseal fusion for cattle from Early Late Saxon Ipswich	28
Table 3.6	Measurements taken on pig bones from Early Late Saxon Ipswich	28
Table 3.7	Epiphyseal fusion data for Early Late Saxon pigs from Ipswich	28
Table 3.8	Measurements taken on Early Late Saxon sheep from Ipswich	29
Table 3.9	Epiphyseal fusion data for Early Late Saxon sheep from Ipswich	31
Table 3.10	Measurements (mm) and withers height estimates (cm) for complete horse long bones from Early Late Saxon Ipswich	31
Table 3.11	Withers height estimates for Early Late Saxon dogs	31
Table 3.12	Measurements on domestic chicken bones from Early Late Saxon Ipswich	32

Middle Late Sxaon

Table 4.1	List of bird and mammal remains recovered from Middle Late Saxon Ipswich	33
Table 4.2	Measurements taken on the Ipswich peregrine falcon compared to those for male and female peregrine falcons	34
Table 4.3	Species ratios for the large domestic mammals from Middle Late Saxon Ipswich	34
Table 4.4	Species ratios for cattle, sheep/goats and pigs from selected Late Saxon sites	35
Table 4.5	Body-part distributions for the large domestic mammals from Middle Late Saxon Ipswich	35
Table 4.6	Epiphyseal fusion data for Middle Late Saxon cattle from Ipswich	37
Table 4.7	Measurement data for Middle Late Saxon cattle from Ipswich	37
Table 4.8	Epiphyseal fusion data for Middle Late Saxon pigs	37
Table 4.9	Measurements taken on pig bones from Middle Late Saxon Ipswich	38
Table 4.10	Measurements taken on sheep/goat remains from Middle Late Saxon Ipswich	38
Table 4.11	Epiphyseal fusion data for Middle Late Saxon sheep from Ipswich	38
Table 4.12	Measurements taken on complete dog long bones from Middle Late Saxon Ipswich	39
Table 4.13	Measurements taken on chicken bones from Middle Late Saxon Ipswich	39

Early Medieval

Table 5.1	Mammal and bird species identified from Early Medieval sites in Ipswich	41
Table 5.2	Species ratios for the large domestic mammals from Early Medieval sites in Ipswich	
Table 5.3	Body-part distributions for the large domestic mammals from Early Medieval Ipswich	42
Table 5.4	Measurements taken on cattle bones from Early Medieval Ipswich	43
Table 5.5	Ageing data for Early Medieval cattle based on epiphyseal fusion of the long bones	45
Table 5.6	Measurements taken on pig bones from Early Medieval Ipswich	45
Table 5.7	Epiphyseal fusion data for Early Medieval pigs from Ipswich	45
Table 5.8	Epiphyseal fusion data for Early Medieval sheep from Ipswich	46
Table 5.9	Measurements taken on sheep/goat bones from Early Medieval Ipswich	46
Table 5.10	Measurements taken on Early Medieval dog bones from Ipswich	47
Table 5.11	Measurements taken on domestic chicken bones from Early Medieval Ipswich	47

Appendix

Table A1	Species list for St Peter's Street Ipswich (5203) Early Middle Saxon	54
Table A2	Species list for Foundation Street/Wingfield Ipswich (4601) Middle Saxon/Early Late Saxon	54
Table A3	Species list for Tower Ramparts Ipswich (0802) Late Medieval	54
Table A4	Species list for Bridge Street Ipswich (6202) Late Medieval	54
Table A5	Species list for St George's Street Ipswich (9802) Late Medieval	55
Table A6	Species list for Foundation Street/Wingfield Ipswich (4601) Late Medieval	55
Table A7	Species list for Tower Ramparts Ipswich (0802) Late Medieval/Early Post-Medieval	55
Table A8	Species list for Bridge Street Ipswich (6202) Late Medieval/Early Post-Medieval	55

Table A9   Species list for Bridge Street Ipswich
           (6202) Post-Medieval   55

Table A10 Amphibian remains from Saxon and
           Medieval contexts at Ipswich   55

Acknowledgements

This volume would not have been possible without the help and support of many people. I am grateful to Sebastian Payne who invited me to work on the Ipswich animal bone materials and to help prepare them for publication. I am also especially indebted to Patricia Stevens who carried out the initial identification and analysis of the mammal bones and to the late Don Bramwell who identified the bird remains. Special thanks are due to Dr Michael Campana, Smithsonian Institution, for the PCA analysis.

The analysis and interpretation of the faunal remains from Ipswich builds on the earlier work that I carried out at the Early Saxon site of West Stow (Crabtree 1982, 1990) and at the Middle Saxon estate centre of Brandon (Crabtree and Campana 2014). The West Stow research was supported by a Fulbright-Hayes Full Grant and renewal to the Archaeology Department at the University of Southampton, a dissertation improvement grant from the US National Science Foundation (Grant Number BNS 77-08141), and a grant from the Wenner-Gren Foundation for Anthropological Research (Grant Number 3267). The work on the Brandon fauna was supported by a summer grant from the US National Endowment for the Humanities (1990). I would like to say a special thank you to Douglas Campana who has worked alongside me on these faunal projects since the 1970s. I am grateful to Jean-Hervé Yvinec who provided important information on the unpublished faunal remains from Quentovic. Thanks are also due to the two anonymous reviewers whose suggestions have made this a better publication. The errors are all mine. Finally, I am grateful to the editors of *East Anglian Archaeology* who made this publication possible.

Preface

This volume is based on the identification and analysis of over 115,000 animal bones and fragments that were recovered from sixteen archaeological sites in Ipswich between 1974 and 1988. These data were part of a larger programme of excavation that was carried out in Ipswich between 1974 and 1990 by the Suffolk Archaeological Unit (subsequently the Suffolk County Council Archaeological Service) under the direction of Keith Wade. The faunal remains were initially identified by my colleague, Patricia Stevens, between 1985 and 1990. I joined the project in 1991 after the completion of the identification of the animal bones from the Middle Saxon site of Brandon in northwest Suffolk (Crabtree 2012; Crabtree and Campana 2014). I was asked to work with Stevens's data to prepare a short report to be included in the Ipswich publication as well as a longer and more detailed archive report.

Unfortunately, work toward the publication of the Ipswich report was delayed and subsequently deferred as a result of the publication of the Planning Policy Guidance 16 document that changed the methods by which archaeological research was funded (Suffolk County Council Archaeological Service 2015). Between 2009 and 2015 an English Heritage-funded project (now Historic England) consolidated the Ipswich archives from 1974 to 1990 and prepared a digital archive. The archive includes the original publication report on the animal bones (Crabtree and Stevens 1994), but the tables and graphs were not included in the on-line version. In addition, the introduction to the digital archive notes that many of the specialist reports are now out-of-date and have not been updated. Some of the Middle Saxon data were published as part of *Middle Saxon Animal Husbandry in East Anglia* (Crabtree 2012), and a few short book chapters on the Ipswich fauna have been published (Crabtree 2016, 2017b, see also Crabtree 2015a), but the vast majority of the data from these 16 sites have never been published. In addition, the available on-line report (Crabtree and Stevens 1994) was written over 25 years ago. At that time, some of the faunal material from Middle Saxon York (O'Connor 1991) had been published, along with the report on the excavations at Melbourne Street in Southampton (Bourdillon and Coy 1980), but almost no data were available from Middle Saxon London. Our 1994 report needs substantial updating to compare the Ipswich data to the other faunal data that are now available from Middle Saxon, Late Saxon and Early Medieval sites that have been excavated in eastern England in the past 25 years, as well as to address changes in zooarchaeological methodology, such as the recognition of traction pathologies (Bartosiewicz *et al.* 1997).

The first chapter of this report will provide a brief background to the archaeology of Ipswich and an introduction to the sites that are included in this volume. The introductory chapter will include an updated discussion of the chronology of Middle Saxon, Late Saxon and Early Medieval Ipswich (*c.* 700–1150). This chapter will also describe the methods used in the study of the faunal remains from Ipswich. The second chapter will focus on the faunal remains from Middle Saxon (*c.* 700–850/880) Ipswich. Ipswich, along with London, York and Saxon Southampton (Hamwic), has been identified as an *emporium* or '*wic*'. These sites are the earliest urban sites in post-Roman Britain, and they served as centres for craft production and trade (Crabtree 2018). Our understanding of the social and economic roles of the *emporia* has changed dramatically in the past 25 years, and the goal of this chapter is to examine the data for urban provisioning at Ipswich in light of these new understandings. Chapters 3 and 4 focus on the Early Late Saxon (*c.* 850/800–900) and Middle Late Saxon (*c.* 900–1000) faunal remains respectively. Chapter 5 will examine the faunal data from Early Medieval Ipswich (*c.* 1000–1150). Unlike the other well-known English '*wic*' sites, Ipswich was continuously occupied from the Middle Saxon through the Early Medieval period. Chapter 6 will examine long-term continuities and changes in urban provisioning at Ipswich from 700 to 1150. The Appendix includes a list of the faunal remains that were recovered from the Early Middle Saxon, Late Medieval and Post-Medieval sites but are not discussed in detail in this volume, as well as a summary of the amphibian remains.

Summary

This volume presents the results of the zooarchaeological analysis of the animal bones that were recovered from sixteen sites in Ipswich between 1974 and 1988. The focus of the study is on the animal bones that were recovered from Middle Saxon (700–850/880), Early Late Saxon (850/880–920), Middle Late Saxon (920–1000) and Early Medieval (1000–1150) sites that were part of the Origins of Ipswich project.

The faunal assemblages from all four periods were composed primarily of cattle, caprines (sheep and goats), pigs, and domestic chickens. Horses were few in number and do not seem to have formed part of the diet after the Middle Saxon period. In terms of NISP (Number of Identified Specimens Per taxon), cattle are always the most numerous animals, followed by pigs and then caprines, but the relative number of sheep and goats increases throughout the Middle Saxon, Late Saxon and Medieval periods. Domestic chickens greatly outnumber domestic geese in all periods. Wild birds and mammals are rare in all the Ipswich assemblages. The most common wild species are red deer (*Cervus elaphus*) and roe deer (*Capreolus capreolus*).

Biometrical data show that the Middle Saxon cattle are comparable in size to the cattle from other Middle Saxon *emporia* in England. These data also suggest that fewer oxen were sent to market in the later periods and that there was a slight overall decrease in the size of cattle by the Early Medieval period. The Middle Saxon sheep from Ipswich are small and comparable in size to the Middle Saxon sheep from rural East Anglian sites such as Brandon in Suffolk. All the Ipswich horses are the size of large ponies; most are between 130 and 140cm (about 13–14 hands) in withers height. The dog remains from the Late Saxon and Early Medieval contexts in Ipswich include dogs of a range of different sizes. The smallest are about 30cm at the withers; the largest are about 50cm in shoulder height.

Ageing data indicate that the inhabitants of Ipswich were supplied with market-aged and older adult cattle, sheep and pigs. Elderly animals and very young animals are rare. These data suggest that the inhabitants of Ipswich obtained their meat from markets throughout the Middle Saxon, Late Saxon and Early Medieval periods.

Résumé

Ce volume présente les résultats de l'analyse archéozoologique d'ossements d'animaux qui ont été retrouvés dans seize sites de la ville d'Ipswich entre 1974 et 1988. Pour l'essentiel, cette étude porte sur des ossements d'animaux provenant de sites de la période saxonne moyenne (700–850/880), du début de la période saxonne tardive (850/880–920), du milieu de la période moyenne tardive (920–1000) et du début de la période médiévale (1000–1150). Ces différents sites font partie du projet Origins of Ipswich.

Les ensembles fauniques des quatre périodes étaient principalement composées de bovins, de caprinés (moutons et chèvres), de porcs et de poules domestiques. Les chevaux étaient peu nombreux et il semble qu'ils ne faisaient pas partie du régime alimentaire après la période saxonne moyenne. En ce qui concerne le nombre de spécimens identifiés par taxon (NISP), les bovins sont toujours les animaux les plus nombreux; ils sont suivis par les porcs puis par les caprinés. Toutefois, le nombre relatif de moutons et de chèvres augmente pendant la totalité des périodes saxonnes moyenne et tardive, et pendant la période médiévale. Les poules domestiques surpassent largement les oies domestiques à toutes les périodes. Les oiseaux sauvages et les mammifères sont rares dans tous les ensembles fauniques d'Ipswich. Le cerf commun (*Cervus elaphus*) et le chevreuil (*Capreolus capreolus*) représentent les espèces sauvages les plus répandues.

Les données biométriques montrent que, durant la période saxonne moyenne, les bovins d'Ipswich sont comparables en taille aux bovins d'autres emporia situés en Angleterre. Ces données suggèrent également qu'un nombre plus limité de bœufs était destiné au marché dans les périodes plus tardives et qu'il y avait aussi une légère diminution générale de la taille des bovins au début de la période médiévale. Pour la période saxonne moyenne, les moutons d'Ipswich sont petits et ils sont comparables en taille aux moutons des sites ruraux de l'East Anglia tels que Brandon dans le Suffolk. Tous les chevaux d'Ipswich ont la taille de grands poneys; ils mesurent ainsi entre 130 et 140cm (environ 13–14 mains) au garrot. On trouve des chiens de tailles différentes parmi les restes d'Ipswich qui proviennent de contextes de la période saxonne tardive et de la période médiévale. Les chiens les plus petits mesurent environ 30cm au garrot et les plus grands environ 50cm à hauteur d'épaule.

Des donnés relatives aux âges indiquent qu'Ipswich était approvisionné en moutons, en porcs et en bovins. Ceux-ci étaient en âge d'être vendus sur les marchés et on trouvait aussi des bovins adultes plus âgés. Les animaux âgés et très jeunes étaient rares. Ces données suggèrent que les habitants d'Ipswich se procuraient leur viande sur les marchés au cours des périodes saxonnes moyenne et tardive et au début de la période médiévale.

(Traduction: Didier Don)

Zusammenfassung

Der vorliegende Band enthält die Ergebnisse der archäozoologischen Analyse der Tierknochen, die zwischen 1974 und 1988 an sechzehn Stätten in Ipswich gefunden wurden. Im Mittelpunkt der Studie stehen die Tierknochen von Stätten aus der mittelangelsächsischen (700–850/880), der frühen spätangelsächsischen (850/880–920), der mittleren spätangelsächsischen (920–1000) und der frühmittelalterlichen (1000–1150) Periode im Rahmen des Projekts Origins of Ipswich.

Die Faunenkomplexe aus allen vier Perioden bestanden vorwiegend aus Rindern, Schafen und Ziegen, Schweinen und Haushühnern. Die Zahl der Pferde, die nach der mittelangelsächsischen Periode offenbar nicht mehr Teil der Nahrung waren, war gering. Mit Blick auf das Taxon Number of Identified Specimens Per, kurz NISP, waren Rinder zahlenmäßig jeweils am stärksten vertreten, gefolgt von Schweinen und danach Schafen und Ziegen, allerdings erhöhte sich die relative Zahl der Schafe und Ziegen im Verlauf der mittelangelsächsischen sowie der spätangelsächsischen und der mittelalterlichen Periode. Die Zahl der Haushühner übertraf die der Hausgänse in allen Perioden deutlich. Wildvögel und Säugetiere sind in allen Ipswich-Fundkomplexen selten. Die am häufigsten vorkommenden Wildtiergattungen sind Rotwild (*Cervus elaphus*) und Rehwild (*Capreolus capreolus*).

Biometrische Daten zeigen, dass die Rinder der mittelangelsächsischen Periode eine vergleichbare Größe aufwiesen wie die in anderen mittelangelsächsischen Emporien in England. Die Daten deuten ferner darauf hin, dass in den späteren Perioden weniger Ochsen auf den Markt getrieben wurden und dass die Größe der Rinder zu Beginn der frühmittelalterlichen Zeit insgesamt leicht zurückgegangen war. Die mittelangelsächsischen Schafe aus Ipswich sind eher klein; sie ähneln größenmäßig den mittelangelsächsischen Schafen an ländlichen Stätten in East Anglia wie etwa Brandon in Suffolk. Alle Ipswich-Pferde haben die Statur großer Ponys; die meisten weisen ein Stockmaß von 130 bis 140cm auf. Die Hundereste aus den spätangelsächsischen und frühmittelalterlichen Fundverbänden in Ipswich zeigen, dass Hunde ganz unterschiedlicher Größe existierten. Die kleinsten maßen etwa 30cm bis zum Widerrist, die größten hatten eine Schulterhöhe von rund 50crn.

Die Altersdatierung zeigt, dass Ipswich mit marktreifen wie auch älteren ausgewachsenen Rindern, Schafen und Schweinen versorgt wurde. Ganz alte sowie ganz junge Tiere waren selten. Die Daten legen nahe, dass die Einwohner von Ipswich ihr Fleisch über die gesamte mittelangelsächsische, spätangelsächsische und frühmittelalterliche Periode von Märkten bezogen.

(Übersetzung: Gerlinde Krug)

Chapter 1. Background to the Study of the Ipswich Animal Remains

I. Introduction

This chapter has two purposes. First it will provide a brief overview of the archaeological background to the 1974–1990 excavations at Ipswich. Although the final report on these excavations has not been published (Wade in prep.), the updated excavation archive is now available online, hosted by the Archaeology Data Service. In addition, the sites that formed the basis for this study of animal remains will be identified, and the information that is not included in Chapters 2–5 can be found in an Appendix. A report on the fish bone remains recovered from some of the sites described in this volume was written by Locker and Jones (1983) and is now available through the Archaeology Data Service. A report on the mammals and birds recovered from five additional sites in Ipswich is available online (Jones and Serjeantson 1983). The sites included in this report are Elm Street (3902), Vernon Street (7402), Lower Brook Street (5502), Great Whip Street (7501), and Turrett Lane (4302). The report describes approximately 30,000 animal bones and fragments that were recovered from Middle Saxon, Late Saxon, and Early Medieval contexts at these sites, although the vast majority of the bones were Middle Saxon in date. An earlier archive report (Jones 1979) describes the fish bone remains that were recovered from these sites.

A second goal of this introduction is to describe the zooarchaeological methods that were used in the initial analysis and identification of the bird and mammal remains from Ipswich. Archaeological and zooarchaeological methods have changed dramatically in the past 30 years because of the availability of more powerful personal computers, the availability of GIS (Geographical Information Systems) technology, and the availability of new methods of study including isotopic analyses and aDNA studies. While it is not possible to apply these new methods to our dataset, the available data on Middle Saxon, Late Saxon, and Early Medieval faunal assemblages is much richer than what was available 30 years ago. It is therefore possible to situate the faunal data from Ipswich within a wider comparative framework.

II. Archaeological Context: Excavations at Ipswich

Although the final report on the excavations from Ipswich has not yet been published, a number of interim reports are available (see Wade 1988a, 1988b, 1993, 2001). In addition, an overview of the history and excavations at Ipswich is provided by Wade (n.d.), and an up-to-date discussion of the chronology is available online (Wade 2013). The discussion presented here is based primarily on Wade (n.d.), and the chronology is based on Wade (2013) (see Table 1.1).

Although some initial work on Ipswich archaeology was carried out during the late 19th and early 20th centuries, the modern history of archaeological research in Ipswich begins in the 1950s. John Hurst and Stanley West studied the sizeable collection of medieval pottery that was housed in Ipswich Museum in the late 1950s. They identified an early form of medieval pottery termed Ipswich ware which they dated to the Middle Saxon period (*c.* AD 650–850) and a later form of pottery that was called Thetford ware because it was initially identified there, although it is now clear that it was also made in Ipswich. Thetford ware was initially dated to *c.* AD 850–1150 (Hurst and West 1957). Stanley West subsequently carried out the first modern excavations in Ipswich at Cox Lane in 1958 and at Shire Hall in 1959 (West 1963). His research demonstrated that Anglo-Saxon Ipswich was a large settlement, covering at least 30ha. By the early 1970s, it was clear that Ipswich was one of a number of urban trading centres known as *emporia* or '*wics*' that were centres of craft production and trade (Hodges 1982, 1989, 2012, see also Crabtree 2018).

The threat that urban redevelopment posed to Suffolk's archaeological heritage, and particularly to Ipswich's Anglo-Saxon and medieval heritage, led to the formation of the Suffolk County Archaeological Unit in 1974. Keith Wade was chosen as the urban archaeologist for the unit and was responsible for monitoring the development of urban sites within the County of Suffolk. The rescue archaeology within the town of Ipswich was part of a larger project, known as the Origins of Ipswich Project, that included the excavation of threatened sites within Ipswich as well as the documentation of standing medieval buildings and the examination of historical records. Between 1974 and 1990, 36 archaeological excavations were carried out within Ipswich, including 27 within the Anglo-Saxon and medieval walls and 9 within the suburbs. This report includes an analysis of the animal bone remains from 16 of these sites.

Early Middle Saxon Ipswich (*c.* AD 600–700)

The settlement of Ipswich was initially established in the 7th century. The earliest occupation includes a settlement north of the Orwell River crossing at Stoke Bridge and a cemetery located on higher ground south of the Buttermarket. The cemetery yielded the remains of 71 men, women and children, including some burials that may have been mounded. A number of the burials included wooden containers including two possible boat burials. A small number of Merovingian individuals from the Continent may have been buried in the cemetery. The results of this excavation have been completely published (Scull 2009). The associated settlement yielded two sunken-featured buildings and rubbish pits containing handmade pottery and imported Frankish wares. The initial settlement and cemetery are dated to the Early Middle Saxon period (c. AD 600–700).

The 7th century is a major period of social, political and economic transition in East Anglia, and more broadly in Northwest Europe. In addition to the establishment of a trading settlement at Ipswich, the royal cemetery at nearby Sutton Hoo (Carver 2005) points to increasing social and economic stratification, especially when it is compared to the earlier cemetery at Tranmer House (Fern 2015). Recent survey and archaeological excavations at Rendlesham indicate that it was a large Early to Middle Saxon settlement from the 5th through the 8th century, with its peak importance dated from the early to mid 6th century through the early 8th century (Scull *et al.* 2016, 1601). The site has been interpreted as a high status farm, residence and tribute centre (Scull *et al.* 2016, 1605), and it may represent the royal vill (*vicus regius*) at Rendlesham that is mentioned by Bede. The site also yielded early evidence for the use of coinage, which became widespread at Ipswich after about AD 720. The development of Early Middle Saxon and Middle Saxon Ipswich needs to be interpreted in light of the larger changes that were taking place in southeast England during the 'long eighth century' (Hansen and Wickham 2000), including increased regional and international trade, more widespread use of coinage, and evidence for increased social and economic complexity with the emergence of the Anglo-Saxon kingdoms (see, for example, Crabtree 2017a).

Middle Saxon Ipswich (AD 700–850/880)
Around AD 700 the town of Ipswich expanded to cover around 50ha. The expansion took place over the heathland to the north of the 7th-century settlement and included a newly established gridded street plan that was centered on the marketplace at the Corn Hill. The buildings in the centre of town were closely packed and positioned up against the street frontage. The backyards of these houses yielded evidence for craft production. The buildings on the eastern edge of the town were more widely spaced and seem to have been associated with agriculture and animal husbandry.

The economy of the Middle Saxon town was based on craft production and international trade. Of particular importance was the production of Ipswich ware, the first industrially produced pottery in Britain since the end of the Roman period. Ipswich ware was fired in kilns and finished on a slow wheel. As noted above, Hurst and West (1957) initially dated the beginnings of the Ipswich ware industry to about AD 650. Detailed research carried out on Ipswich ware since the 1990s (Blinkhorn 1999; 2012), suggests that the Ipswich pottery industry was probably established a half-century later, in the early 8th century, while scientific dating of the Ipswich ware kiln recently discovered at Stoke Quay suggests a date nearer 700 (Brown *et al.* 2020, 419). Other craft activities practiced in the town included bone- and antler-working, textile production and metal-working. Evidence for leather-working has been recovered from waterlogged deposits near the waterfront. The evidence for substantial craft specialisation within Middle Saxon Ipswich is important, since craft-workers must have obtained their meat and other animal products from rural producers. The question of how this meat was obtained is a major focus of this volume.

Period	Dates	Ceramic Assemblage
Early Middle Saxon	AD 600-700	Handmade wares
Middle Saxon	AD 700-850/880	Ipswich ware and continental imports
Early Late Saxon	AD 850/880-900	Thetford ware, decreased Ipswich ware
Middle Late Saxon	AD 900-1000	Thetford ware, St Neots ware
Early Medieval	AD 1000-1150	Early Medieval wares

Table 1.1 Chronological framework for the Ipswich excavations, based on Wade (2013)

The other striking feature of Middle Saxon Ipswich is the evidence for international trade. Over 6000 imported pottery sherds representing 900 vessels were recovered from the 1974–90 excavations in Ipswich. This pottery was produced in the Rhineland, Belgium and northern France, and much of it was probably used by continental traders who were resident in Ipswich. Other imported goods include lava querns from the Rhineland and hone stones from Norway.

Similar evidence for craft production and trade has been recovered from Middle Saxon London (Lundenwic), Middle Saxon Southampton (Hamwic), and Middle Saxon York (Eorforwic). These early urban centres are known as *emporia* or '*wics*' and have been compared to similar sites on the Continent, such as Quentovic in France and Dorestad in the Netherlands. Hodges (1982) initially suggested that these sites were used by emerging Anglo-Saxon kings to control the distribution of prestige items from the Continent. More recent research has emphasised the role of regional trade (Moreland 2001) and has emphasised the importance of the *emporia* as places where trade could be concentrated and taxed (see, for example, Crabtree 2018, Hodges 2012).

Early Late Saxon Ipswich (*c.* AD 850/880–900)
From a political perspective, this period corresponds to the time when Ipswich came under Viking control. Ipswich first came under Viking control in 880 and it returned to West Saxon control in 920. During this period, Ipswich ware was gradually replaced by Thetford ware. Ipswich was surrounded by defences for the first time during the Early Late Saxon period, and sunken-featured buildings were introduced as well. There is a marked increase in craft activities, including iron-smithing and copper-alloy metal-working.

Middle Late Saxon Ipswich (*c.* AD 900–1000)
This period is marked by the production of both Thetford ware and St Neots ware. It broadly corresponds to the period when Ipswich was once again under Anglo-Saxon control after 920. Ipswich remained one of the ten largest towns in Britain during this period. The town layout of this period became more uniform, with buildings set back 10–15m from the street frontage. The sunken-featured structures of the Early Middle Saxon period developed into two-storey dwellings, with the sunken portion serving as a cellar or half-basement. Similar architectural changes were also seen in York during this period (Hall 1994, 59–60). The economy of Ipswich continued to be based on craft production and trade, and the town obtained

a mint under King Edgar (r. AD 959–975). Most of the 10th-century trade appears to have been local and regional, rather than international.

Early Medieval Ipswich (*c.* AD 1000–1150)
This period is marked by the replacement of Anglo-Saxon pottery by early medieval wares. There is no break in the occupation of Ipswich between the Middle Late Saxon and Early Medieval periods. In political terms this period spans the end of the Anglo-Saxon period and the first century after the Norman Conquest. Other researchers have used the term Saxo-Norman to refer to 11th- and early 12th-century sites in Britain. While international trade increased in the 11th century, the town of Ipswich suffered after the Norman Conquest. In the late 11th century, about three-quarters of the urban plots lay in waste, and only about one-quarter of the burgesses were able to pay their dues to the king. By the end of this period, Ipswich was only the 21st largest town in England. This urban decline is probably the result of the suppression of a revolt against William the Conqueror by the Earl of East Anglia in 1075.

III. Materials and Methods

This volume describes 115,998 animal bones and fragments that were recovered from 16 sites in Ipswich between 1974 and 1988. The 16 sites discussed here range in date from the Early Middle Saxon period through the high Middle Ages and the post-medieval period. The vast majority of the faunal remains recovered date to the Middle Saxon, Early Late Saxon, Middle Late Saxon, and Early Medieval periods. The bone from the later medieval and post-medieval periods was not part of the research aims of the 1974–90 excavation project; however the bones are available for future study. The sample of bones chosen for analysis was biased toward the Saxon assemblages. These fauna can provide vital background information on the economic foundations of Ipswich. In addition, pottery indicates that residuality is a greater problem for the later contexts at Ipswich. The Saxon and Early Medieval faunal samples are less likely to be contaminated by non-contemporary faunal material.

The animal bones recovered from the Middle Saxon, Early Late Saxon, Middle Late Saxon, and Early Medieval contexts are summarised in Chapters 2–5. The bones recovered from other periods are included in a brief Appendix. The location of the sites included in this study is shown in Figure 1.1, and a brief description of the faunal assemblage from each site is provided below. This information was provided to Pat Stevens by Keith Wade.

- The Foundation Street/Star Lane site **(5801)** produced materials from the Middle Saxon and Early Medieval periods. In addition to the unmodified animal bones evidence of antler-working is present in the faunal assemblages from both periods.

- The Arcade Street site **(1804)** produced faunal materials from both the Early Late Saxon and the Early Medieval periods.

- The Tower Ramparts site **(0802)** produced animal bones recovered from pits dating to the Middle Saxon, Early Late Saxon, Middle Late Saxon, Early Medieval and Late Medieval periods. The identified animal bones from the Late Medieval and Early Post-Medieval assemblages are summarised in Appendix Tables A3 and A7.

- The Little Whip Street site **(7404)** faunal assemblage is made up of bones that were recovered by flotation from a Middle Saxon pit.

- The faunal assemblage from the Tacket Street site **(3410)** includes animal bone material from the Early Late Saxon, Middle Late Saxon, and Early Medieval periods. One feature from each period at the site was sieved and subjected to flotation. Some worked bone material was recovered from one Late Saxon feature.

- The animal bones recovered from the Bridge Street **(6202)** site came mainly from one large trench. The faunal remains include animal bones from the Middle Saxon, Early Late Saxon, Middle Late Saxon, Early Medieval, Late Medieval, Late Medieval/Early Post-Medieval, and Post-Medieval periods. Antler waste, worked bone, and a large number of goat horn cores were recovered from all Saxon periods at the site. The Late Medieval and Post-Medieval faunal remains are summarised in Appendix Tables A4, A8, and A9.

- The St Peter's Street site **(5202)** produced animal bones from the Middle Saxon, Early Late Saxon, and Middle Late Saxon periods. Antler waste was also recovered from this site.

- The Key Street site **(5901)** yielded animal bones from the Middle Saxon, Early Late Saxon, Middle Late Saxon, and Early Medieval periods as well as waste from antler- and horn-working

- The Shire Hall Yard site **(6904)** produced faunal remains from the Middle and Middle Late Saxon periods.

- The Fore Street site **(5902)** produced a small collection of animal bones from Early Medieval features.

- The Buttermarket/St Stephen's Lane site **(3104)** yielded animal bones from the Middle Saxon, Early Late Saxon, Middle Late Saxon, and Early Medieval periods.

- The St Nicholas Street site **(4201)** yielded animal bones from the Early Late Saxon, Middle Late Saxon, and Early Medieval periods. All features at the site produced large quantities of antler waste, goat horn cores, and some worked bone.

- Animal bone fragments, including a large number of goat horn cores, were recovered from the St George's Street site **(9802)**, mainly from Late Medieval contexts. These data are summarised in the Appendix Table A5.

- The Foundation Street/School Lane site **(4801)** yielded a sizeable assemblage of animal bones from Middle Saxon, Early Late Saxon, Middle Late Saxon, and Early Medieval contexts.

- A substantial faunal assemblage was recovered from the Middle Saxon features at the Foundation Street/Wingfield Street site **(4601)**. Additional faunal remains were recovered from the Middle Saxon/Early Late Saxon, Early Late Saxon, Middle Late Saxon,

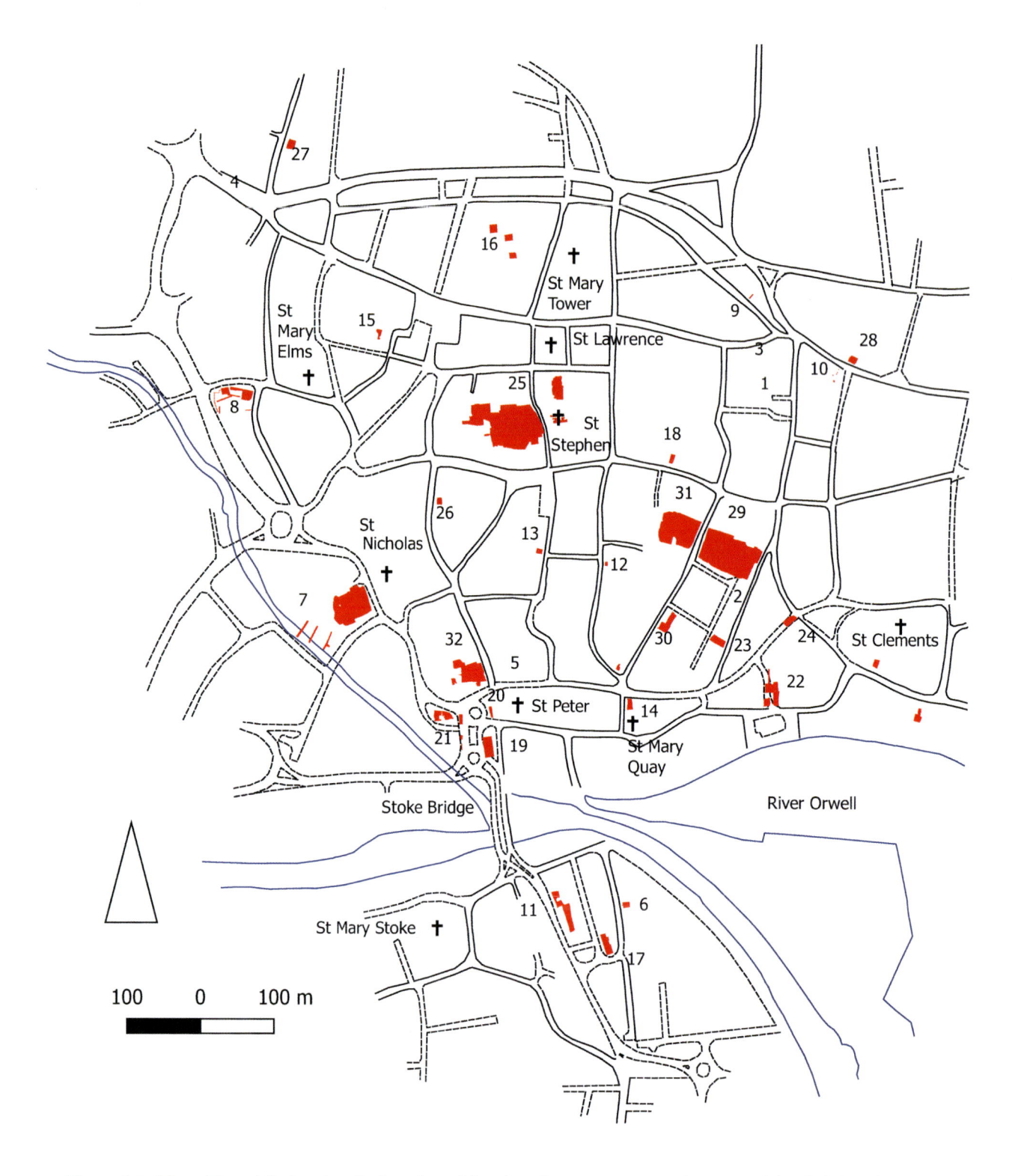

Figure 1.1 Map of Ipswich showing the location of the sites that were excavated as part of the Origins of Ipswich project. The sites included in this study are:

14. Foundation Street/Star Lane (5801)
15. Arcade Street (1804)
16. Tower Ramparts (0802)
17. Little Whip Street (7404)
18. Tacket Street (3410)
19. Bridge Street (6202)
20. St Peter's Street (5202)
22. Key Street (5901)
23. Shire Hall Yard (6904)
24. Fore Street (5902)
25. Buttermarket (3104)
26. St Nicholas Street (4201)
27. St George's Street (9802)
29. Foundation Street/School Lane (4801)
31. Foundation Street/Wingfield (4601)
32. St Peter's Street (5203)

4

Early Medieval, and Late Medieval periods. The material from the Middle Saxon/Early Late Saxon and Late Medieval periods are summarised in Appendix Tables A2 and A6.

- A sample of animal bones from selected features was examined from the St Peter's Street site **(5203)**. The bones include material from the Early Middle Saxon, Middle Saxon, Early Late Saxon, Middle Late Saxon, and Early Medieval periods. The identified Early Middle Saxon remains are summarised in Appendix Table A1.

The Ipswich animal bones were initially identified by Patricia Stevens between 1985 and 1990. The bird remains were identified by the late Don Bramwell. At that time, computer databases for archaeozoology and computer hardware and software were not nearly as powerful and sophisticated as they are today. Stevens entered the data on 8-line punch tape, and these data were subsequently stored on reels of magnetic tape and sorted using a minicomputer. The system was initially developed by R.T. Jones of the former Ancient Monuments Laboratory in London (Jones 1976). At a meeting held in the fall of 1977, Roger Jones, Jennie Coy, Mark Maltby, Douglas Campana and I expanded the codes used in the system to allow analysts to record the full suite of measurements defined by von den Driesch (1976) and to permit more detailed methods of dental ageing following Grant (1976, see also Grant 1982). Additional anatomical codes, as well as information on bone condition and fragmentation, were added at this time. This system was also used to record the original data from Anglo-Saxon West Stow (Crabtree 1982, 1990, see also Crabtree 2014) as well as a number of other large faunal projects that were carried out by Mark Maltby and Jennie Coy at the Southampton University faunal remains unit (e.g., Coy and Maltby 1991).

The development of more powerful personal computers since the 1990s has made the Ancient Monuments Laboratory system obsolete. Today most zooarchaeologists record their data using commercial database managers (e.g., Microsoft Access), specialised database managers (e.g., FAUNA, see Campana 2010), and/or commercial spreadsheet programs (e.g., Microsoft Excel). These programs allow the zooarchaeological data to be shared with other researchers and also allow the data themselves to be published. One goal of this report is to provide zooarchaeological data that can be used by other researchers.

The other problem with the original Ipswich faunal data is that the descriptive data on butchery, dental ageing, and paleopathology were recorded using a series of string codes. For example, the data on butchery used a series of codes in a single string that described the location of the mark, the nature of the mark, and the direction of the mark. This approach makes it difficult to combine the butchery data in any meaningful way. Today most researchers use separate fields to describe these variables (see, for example, Seetah 2018).

Other data that were recorded using the AML system included species, anatomical element, portion of the bone and degree of fragmentation, and epiphyseal fusion of the long bones. Higher order taxa, such as sheep/goat and small artiodactyl, were used to describe bones that could not be identified to species. As noted above, measurements were recorded following the recommendations of von den Driesch (1976), and withers heights were estimated using the factors recommended by von den Driesch and Boessneck (1974).

One major limitation of the data is that the post-cranial remains of sheep and goat were not consistently distinguished using the criteria established by Boessneck *et al.* (1964; see also Boessneck 1969, Halstead *et al.* 2002, Zeder and Lapham 2010, Zeder and Pilaar 2010). Very few of the sheep and goat post-cranial bones were identified to species. Most of the bones that were identified to species were sheep and goat horn cores. The identified skull and horn core remains indicate that sheep outnumber goats in the Ipswich faunal assemblage by a ratio of nearly 2 to 1. It is likely, however, that the cranial remains dramatically over-represent the number of goats in the overall faunal sample, since male goat horns were commonly used in horn-working industries at *emporium* sites (see, for example, Bourdillon and Coy 1980, 97, 111). Although sizeable numbers of male goat horn cores were recovered from Hamwic, the post-cranial remains included very few goat bones. The goats that were identified were generally larger than the Hamwic sheep. For example the sheep metatarsal distal breadth (Bd) at Hamwic ranged from 20.1 to 25.4mm (n = 50, mean = 23.8, s = 1.1), while the goat metatarsal distal breadth ranged from 25.6 to 28.3mm (n = 4) (Bourdillon and Coy 1977, 12). The measurements on the caprine bones from Ipswich are generally small and show a low co-efficient of variation. I therefore assume that most of the post-cranial and dental/mandibular caprine remains from Ipswich represent sheep rather than goats. At other Anglo-Saxon sites where sheep and goats were systematically distinguished, including West Stow (Crabtree 1990), and Brandon (Crabtree and Campana 2014), goats make up a very small percentage of the overall faunal collections (see also Crabtree and Campana 2017).

- Despite the drawbacks, the rich mammal and bird assemblage from Ipswich can be used to answer important questions about urban provisioning and the roles of both animal husbandry and hunting in the Anglo-Saxon diet. These include the following questions:

- What roles did animal husbandry and hunting play in the Saxon and Early Medieval diet in Ipswich?

- What was the relative importance of cattle, pigs and caprines in the Ipswich diet?

- How large were the domestic animals, and is there evidence for changes in animal size through time?

- How old were the animals that formed part of the diet at Ipswich?

- How does the zooarchaeological evidence from Ipswich compare to other early medieval towns in Britain and on the Continent?

- Did the inhabitants of Ipswich obtain their meat through markets, or were they provisioned in more indirect ways, such as by food rents?

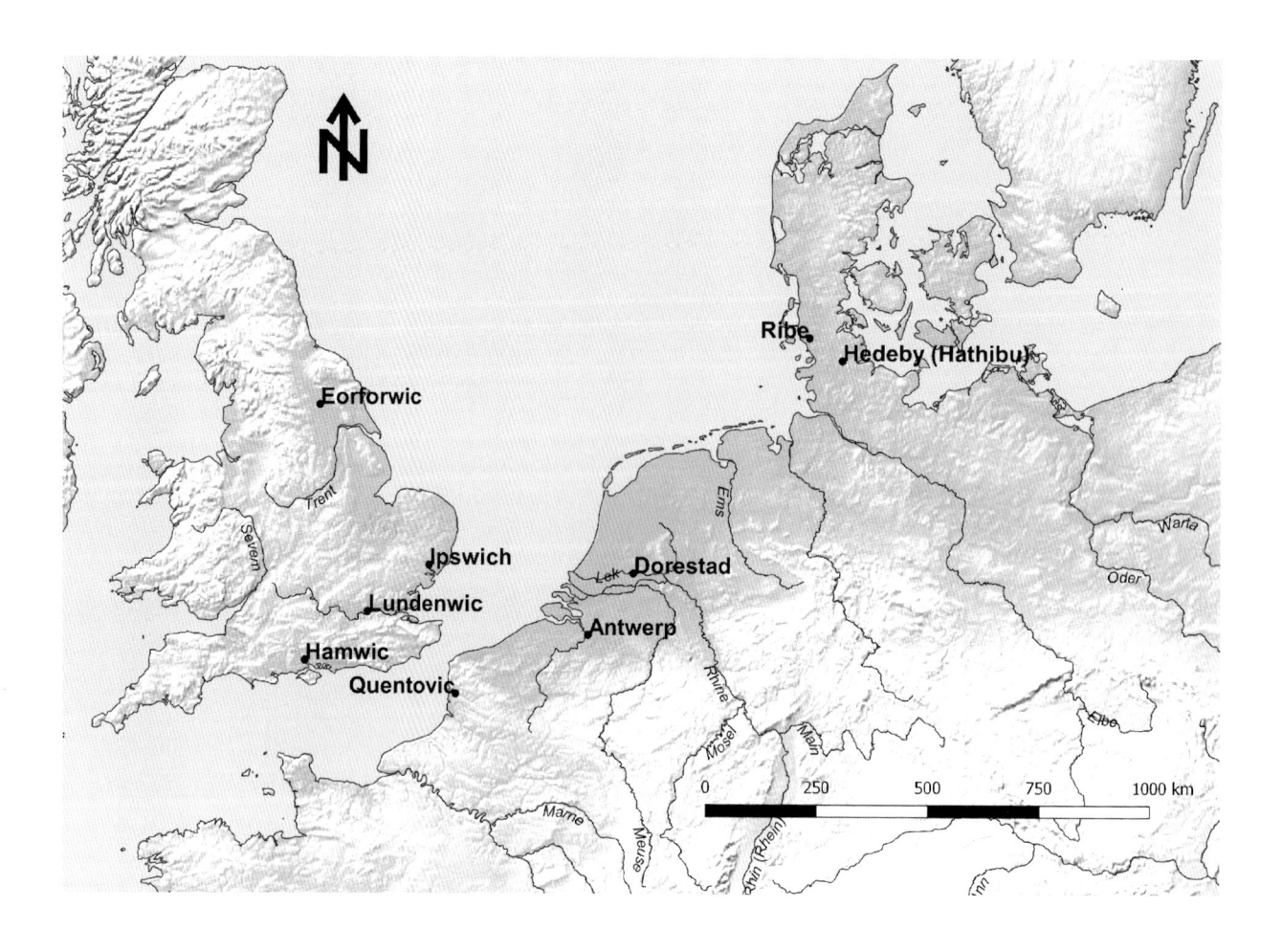

Figure 2.1 Map of eastern England and northwest Europe showing the sites discussed in this volume

Chapter 2. Animal Bones from Middle Saxon Ipswich

I. Introduction

This chapter presents the zooarchaeological data recovered from eleven Middle Saxon sites in Ipswich. Some of these data were presented in *Middle Saxon Animal Husbandry in East Anglia* (Crabtree 2012), but the goal of that volume was to compare the data from Middle Saxon Ipswich to the rich archaeological records from rural Middle Saxon sites in East Anglia, including Brandon in Suffolk (Tester *et al.* 2014) and Wicken Bonhunt in Essex (Wade 1980). The goal of this chapter is to examine the zooarchaeological data on urban provisioning from the earliest urban horizons at Ipswich and to compare these data to the zooarchaeological data from other contemporary early urban centres in Britain and on the Continent. To do this, this chapter will begin with a brief discussion of the '*wic*' or *emporium* sites and their roles in 7th–9th-century Northwest Europe.

II. The Archaeology of the '*Wics*'

The *emporia* have played a major role in study of early medieval urbanism since the early 1980s. In the early part of the 20th century, the great Belgian medieval historian, Henri Pirenne (1925), argued that Roman urbanism and trade patterns continued in Western Europe until the spread of Islam across the Mediterranean in the 8th century. This severed the trade contacts between the Mediterranean and Northwest Europe, leading to the formation of new trade networks and ultimately to the rebirth of towns in medieval Europe. Pirenne's model was based primarily on documentary data, but the emergence of medieval archaeology in the first few decades after the Second World War has provided a wealth of new data on the relationship between towns and trade in early medieval Northwest Europe.

Archaeological, historical and numismatic data indicate that a number of new urban settlements were founded in Northwest Europe along both sides of the North Sea between the 7th and the 9th centuries. Some of the earliest excavations at these *emporia* were carried out at Dorestad in the Netherlands between 1967 and 1977. (See Figure 2.1 for the locations of the sites discussed in this chapter.) The site is located at the point where the lower Rhine River splits into the Lek and the Kromme Rijn. Excavations revealed an area of 30ha that included a harbour, a trading centre, and an agricultural settlement that was located further inland. A large faunal assemblage was recovered from the site (Prummel 1983). Recent numismatic studies (Coupland 2002) indicate that trading activities in Dorestad peaked in the early 9th century and declined rapidly in the 840s and 850s.

Hamwic, Middle Saxon Southampton, was the first of the *emporium* sites in Britain to be excavated systematically. Hamwic, sometimes known as Hamtun, is located on the west bank of the River Itchen, just north of the point where the Test and Itchen Rivers converge. Archaeological work at the Melbourne Street site was carried out between 1971 and 1976 (Holdsworth 1980). Portions of Southampton were quarried for brickearth in the Victorian period, so nearly all the artefactual and faunal material from Melbourne Street was recovered from pits, wells and postholes. The rich zooarchaeological evidence from these excavations was studied by Bourdillon and Coy (1977, 1980), and Bourdillon (1988, 1994) developed a model for the provisioning of Hamwic based on the use of food rents. This model will be discussed in greater detail below.

Subsequent excavations in Hamwic were carried out at the Six Dials site (Andrews 1997). Since this part of the town was not damaged by quarrying for brickearth, the excavations at Six Dials revealed the remains of 60 Middle Saxon buildings and evidence for the street plan of Hamwic during the 8th and 9th centuries. The houses were generally 4–5m wide and up to 10m long, and some buildings appear to be combined homes and workshops (Brisbane 1994, 31). The streets were laid out in a rectilinear grid, and Hamwic may have been home to between 2000 and 3000 people during the Middle Saxon period (Andrews 1997, 253).

Drawing on his own research on the imported pottery from Hamwic, as well as numismatic and historical evidence, Hodges (1982; see also Hodges 1989, 2012) developed a model for the origins and functions of the *emporia*. He linked the appearance of the '*wic*' sites to broader processes of urbanisation and state formation in medieval Europe, arguing that the '*wic*' sites were used by Anglo-Saxon kings to control the trade in imported high-status items from the European Continent. This model is an example of a 'prestige goods' model (Friedman and Rowlands 1977) that suggests emerging elites can gain political and economic power through the control of high quality goods that are made of expensive and often imported materials.

Archaeological research that has been carried out since the early 1980s at the *emporia* and other Middle Saxon sites has challenged Hodges' original model. In 1997 the Portable Antiquities Scheme (PAS) was initiated to encourage members of the public, including metal detectorists, to report the archaeological finds that they encounter. The Portable Antiquities Scheme has led to the identification of a number of Middle Saxon 'productive sites' in eastern England (Pestell and Ulmschneider 2003; Ulmschneider 2000). These sites have produced substantial quantities of metal items, including coins, copper-alloy items, and other non-ferrous metal objects. These sites are located near major land or water routes and seem to be centres of commerce, such as local markets or fairs. In addition, recent numismatic studies of Anglo-Saxon coinage indicate that the Middle Saxon economy was partially monetised (Naismith 2012), providing more evidence for local and regional trade. Intensive archaeological surveys on both sides of the North Sea (Loveluck and Tys 2006) have identified numerous small trading places dated to between AD 600 and 1000 on both the English and the continental coasts. These data point to substantial local, regional and international trade during the Middle Saxon period, and it is very unlikely that the Anglo-Saxon kings had the ability to control this trade. Instead, the creation of the '*wic*' sites may have allowed the emerging Anglo-Saxon monarchs to concentrate and tax trade (for a more complete discussion, see Crabtree 2018 and the references sited therein).

Excavations at Eorforwic (Middle Saxon York) were carried out by the York Archaeological Trust between 1985 and 1986. The excavators have used the term Anglian to describe the 8th–9th-century archaeological material from York. I have used the term Middle Saxon here for consistency. The Fishergate site, which was occupied between the late 7th or early 8th century and the 860–870s, was identified as a '*wic*' based on archaeological, historical and place-name evidence (Kemp 1996, 64–66). The site covered between 26 and 65ha, and it appears to have been home to between 1000 and 1500 people (Hamerow 2007, 223). In addition to evidence for craft specialisation and trade, the Fishergate site yielded a large and well-preserved faunal assemblage that was analysed by Terry O'Connor (1991) of York University. This assemblage serves as an important comparandum for the data from Middle Saxon Ipswich.

At the time that the Origins of Ipswich Project began in 1974, the location of Lundenwic (Middle Saxon London) had not yet been identified. Writing in the 8th century, Bede noted that a market for all nations existed in London, but the location of the Middle Saxon settlement and trading centre was not identified until 1984. Working independently, Martin Biddle (1984) and Alan Vince (1984, see also Vince 1990, 13–25) used the distribution of Middle Saxon pottery, coins and other artifacts, along with place-name and topographic evidence, to show that Lundenwic was located about 1km upstream from the old walled Roman city of Londinium. A number of excavations have been carried out in Middle Saxon London since the 1980s, but the most important is the excavation that was carried out at the Royal Opera House from 1989–1999. This 2500m² excavation yielded important information on the layout of the Middle Saxon settlement, as well as a rich and well-collected faunal assemblage (Rielly 2003). Sixty Middle Saxon buildings were excavated at the Opera House site, and excavations provided substantial evidence for craft production and trade. Organisation of the crafts was based on a model of 'cooperative diversity' (Malcolm and Bowsher 2003, xv) where related trades such as knife-makers and bone-workers who made the handles for the knives were located close to one another. Lundenwic appears to have been the largest of the '*wic*' sites with an estimated Middle Saxon population of 6,000–7,000 people (Cowie *et al.* 2012, 116).

An enormous collection of faunal material has also been recovered from excavations at Haithabu/Hedeby in the region of Schleswig-Holstein, northern Germany. This early medieval town is located on a navigable inlet of the Schlei River that connects to the Baltic Sea. The site is only about 15km east of the Treene River which flows into the Eider and then into the North Sea. It is therefore well located for both north-south and east-west trade during the early medieval period. Haithabu was founded in the late 8th century, and it first appears in the historical record in the Frankish Chronicles of Einhard in 804. Haithabu served as a centre of trade and craft-production until its destruction in 1066. The earlier excavations at the site concentrated on the settlement area, but more recent archaeological research has focused on the harbour.

The animal bone assemblages from Lundenwic, Eorforwic, Hamwic, Dorestad and Haithabu/Hedeby provide the main comparanda for the faunal collections from Middle Saxon Ipswich. Other contemporary '*wic*' sites are known from continental Europe, including Quentovic in France and Ribe in Denmark. The fauna from the excavations at Quentovic are currently under study and have not yet been published. A short paper on the fauna from Ribe was published as part of the report on the 1970–76 excavations (Hatting 1991). The excavations at Ribe yielded about 9000 animal bones and fragments that were recovered from several sites in Ribe that were dated to the 8th century.

One early medieval town that has not been identified as an *emporium* but that has yielded contemporary faunal material is Antwerp. The initial excavations of early medieval Antwerp were carried out in the 1950s before the development of modern methods of archaeological excavation and analysis. The excavation of the Burcht sites in central Antwerp (Bellens *et al.* 2012) provided an opportunity to explore the 8th–10th-century urban foundations of Antwerp. Excavations at the site revealed buildings, wooden trackways, and substantial evidence for craft production, including bone-, antler- and metal-working. Radiocarbon dates show that these early urban deposits date between AD 760 and 970. The excavation strategy focused on the careful recovery of environmental evidence including microstratigraphic data, insect remains and a rich and well-preserved zooarchaeological assemblage (Crabtree *et al.* 2017). The faunal data can serve as an important comparandum for the animal bone remains from Middle and Late Saxon Ipswich.

This chapter will focus on the following questions. What was the nature of the Middle Saxon diet in Ipswich? What roles did animal husbandry and hunting play in the Middle Saxon diet? How were the residents of Middle Saxon Ipswich supplied with meat and other animal products, and what roles may have been played by markets and food rents? And, finally, can the animal bone assemblage from Ipswich tell us anything about the relationship between the '*wic*' and the surrounding countryside?

III. The Composition of the Middle Saxon Faunal Assemblage from Ipswich

A small assemblage of Early Middle Saxon animal bones (Appendix Table A1) was recovered from the St Peter's Street site. The assemblage is dominated by the remains of domestic animals, including cattle, pigs and caprines, along with smaller numbers of domestic chicken, horse and dog bones. Small numbers of red deer and roe deer bones were also recovered from this site, but the deer remains make up only 1.2% of the identified assemblage.

Site No.	5801	0802	7404	6202	5202	5901	6904	4801	4601	5203	3104	Total
Species												
Domestic Mammals												
Cattle (*Bos taurus*)	98	8	3	899	62	27	177	408	595	1842	163	4282
Sheep (*Ovis aries*)	1	1	1	7	4	0	0	2	15	14	1	46
Goat (*Capra hircus*)	1	0	0	3	0	0	2	2	13	18	1	40
Sheep/Goat	136	9	14	305	28	28	65	238	431	720	146	2120
Pig (*Sus scrofa*)	143	13	6	262	37	37	206	223	952	1046	210	3130
Horse (*Equus caballus*)	1	0	0	2	0	0		12	5	40	0	62
Dog (*Canis familiaris*)	0	0	0	1	0	0	0	9	2	4	1	17
Cat (*Felis catus*)	3	0	0	0	25	0	0	0	6	24	4	62
Wild Mammals												
Red Deer (*Cervus elaphus*)	2	0	0	14	0	0	3	1	1	4	2	27
Roe Deer (*Capreolus capreolus*)	0	0	0	0	0	0	0	0	1	10	1	12
Hare (*Lepus* sp.)	0	0	0	0	0	0	0	0	0	1	0	1
Otter (*Lutra lutra*)	0	0	0	0	0	0	0	0	0	1	0	1
Domestic Birds												
Chicken (*Gallus gallus*)	29	5	0	27	7	7	6	95	159	149	33	517
Goose (*Anser anser*)	13	3	0	15	1	1	2	22	0	56	12	126
Wild Birds												
Mallard (*Anas platyrhynchos*)	0	0	0	0	0	0	0	1	1	7	0	9
Swan (*Cygnus olor*)	0	0	0	0	0	0	0	1	0	0	0	1
Pigeons (*Columba* sp.)	0	0	0	0	0	0	0	2	1	0	0	3
Raven (*Corvus corax*)	0	0	0	0	0	0	0	2	0	1	0	1
Jackdaw (*Corvus munedula*)	0	0	0	0	0	0	0	0	3	0	0	3
Crows (*Corvus* sp.)	0	0	0	0	0	0	0	0	0	1	0	2
Gannets (*Morus* sp.)	0	0	0	2	0	0	0	0	0	0	0	2
Total	427	39	24	1537	164	92	463	1017	2184	3939	574	10465

Table 2.1 List of identified bird and mammal remains recovered from eleven Middle Saxon sites in Ipswich

The assemblage is too small to allow detailed comparisons with other 7th-century faunal assemblages from East Anglia, but it is worth noting that both cattle and pigs outnumber caprines in the St Peter's Street assemblage.

Eleven of the archaeological sites studied as part of this project yielded faunal material that could be dated to the Middle Saxon period. Most of this material was recovered from pits. The identified mammal and bird remains that were recovered from these sites are shown in Table 2.1. The four bones of common shrew and a single bone from a short-tailed vole that were recovered from the St Peter's Street site were excluded from the chart, since these animals are unlikely to have played an economic role in Middle Saxon Ipswich. Frog and frog/toad bones were recovered from a number of sites in the town. These are also unlikely to have played an economic role in Saxon and Medieval Ipswich, and they have been summarised in Appendix Table A10.

The Middle Saxon faunal assemblages from Ipswich are dominated by the remains of domestic mammals and birds. Hunted mammals are rare and are limited to small numbers of red deer and roe deer, along with a single bone each of otter and hare. Most of the bird remains are bones of domestic chickens and geese. Wild birds are rare, and the Ipswich assemblage lacks the diverse range of water birds and waders that were present in the faunal assemblages from rural East Anglian sites, including West Stow (Crabtree 1990) and Brandon (Crabtree 2012; Crabtree and Campana 2014). Many of the wild birds that were identified from the Ipswich faunal collection were corvids (members of the crow family), and these birds can thrive in urban conditions since they scavenge human refuse (Marzluff and Angell 2005, 292).

Species ratios based on NISP (Number of Identified Specimens Per taxon, see Lyman 2008) have been calculated for the large domestic mammals (cattle, sheep/goats, pigs and horses) from both the Early Middle Saxon and the Middle Saxon faunal assemblages from Ipswich (Table 2.2 and Figs 2.2 and 2.3). Both assemblages are dominated by cattle, followed by pigs and then caprines. Horses make up a very small percentage of both assemblages, and they were probably not a regular part of the Middle Saxon diet. The main difference between the two assemblages is that cattle are more common in the Early Middle Saxon assemblage. It is not clear whether this represents a real difference or whether this is an artifact of the small sample size of the Early Middle Saxon assemblage. The rank order of the domestic mammals is the same in both assemblages.

To compare the species ratios from Middle Saxon East Anglia to the other Anglo-Saxon *emporia*, the species ratios based on NISP have been recalculated to exclude horse remains and to include only cattle, caprines and pigs. These data (see Table 2.3 and Figure 2.4) show that all the Middle Saxon assemblages from eastern England are dominated by the remains of cattle. However, sheep are second in number at both Hamwic and York, while pigs are more numerous than sheep at both Lundenwic

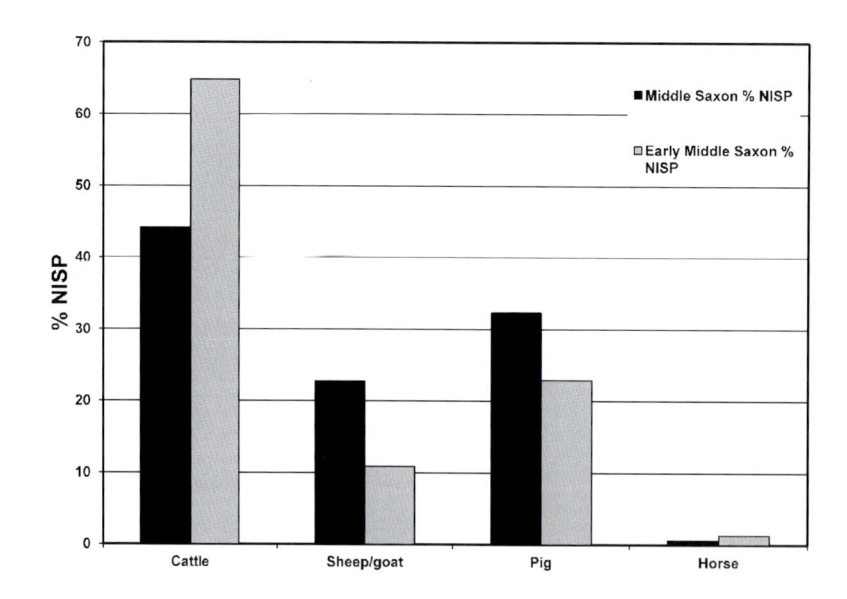

Figure 2.2 Species ratios based on NISP for cattle, sheep/goat, pig and horse remains recovered from Early Middle Saxon and Middle Saxon Ipswich

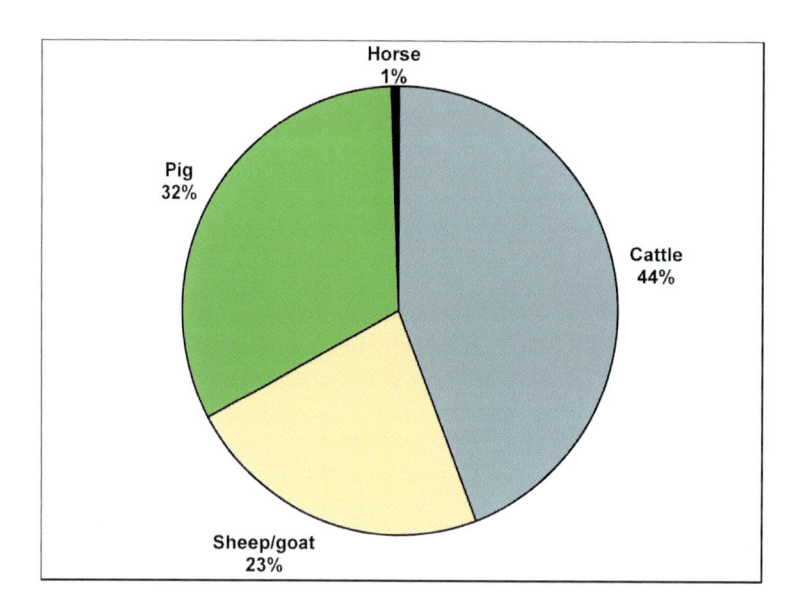

Figure 2.3 Species ratios based on NISP for the cattle, sheep/goat, pig and horse remains from Middle Saxon Ipswich

	EMS NISP	EMS %NISP	MS NISP	MS %NISP
Cattle	302	64.8	4282	44.2
Sheep/goat	51	10.9	2206	22.8
Pig	107	23.0	3130	32.3
Horse	6	1.3	62	0.6

Table 2.2 Species ratios based on NISP calculated for the cattle, sheep/goat, pig and horse remains recovered from Early Middle Saxon and Middle Saxon sites in Ipswich

and Ipswich. Of the four assemblages, Middle Saxon (Anglian) York has the highest proportion of cattle and the fewest pigs, while Ipswich has the fewest cattle and the largest percentage of pigs.

The dominance of cattle at all the '*wic*' sites is not unexpected. The *emporia* were home to substantial numbers of craft-workers who probably did not produce their own food. In terms of urban provisioning, cattle would have provided far more meat per animal that either pigs or sheep. It is worth noting that cattle are the most common species recovered from Roman urban and military sites as well (see, for example, King 1984, King 1999, Hammon 2011). The question of why the Ipswich assemblage also includes a high proportion of pigs is one that deserves some attention. The area around Ipswich is not ideal pig-rearing country. Pigs do best in wood pastures where they can forage for foods such as acorns and beech mast (Jørgensen 2013). However, some pigs could have been kept in and around Ipswich. Pigs can also do well in urban areas where they can survive on human refuse. For example, historical records and archaeological evidence (see Milne and Crabtree 2002) both indicate that pigs were kept in Manhattan (New York City) during the 19th century. There are other parts of eastern England that

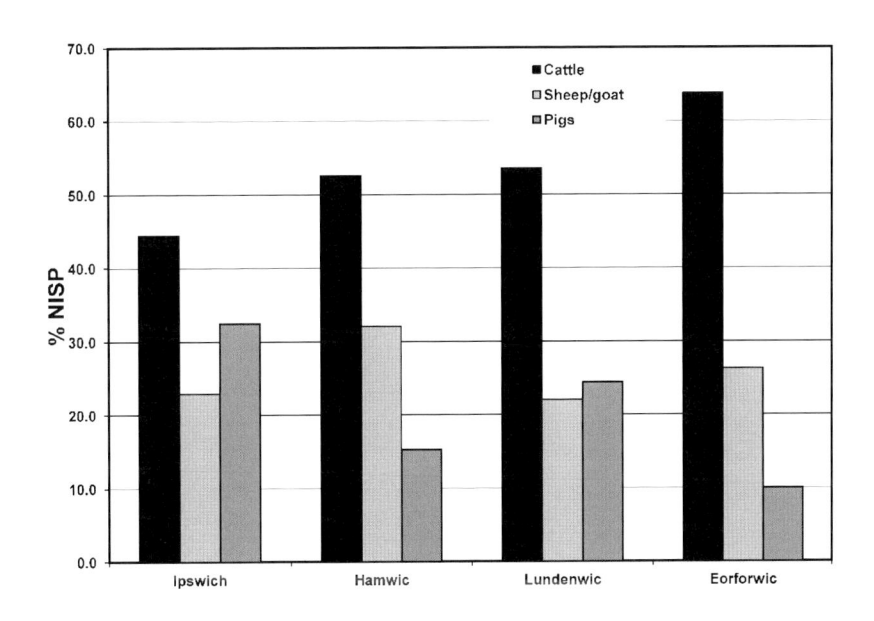

Figure 2.4 Species ratios based on NISP for cattle, sheep/goats and pigs from Middle Saxon Hamwic, York, Lundenwic (Opera House site), and Ipswich

	Ipswich	Hamwic	Lundenwic	Eorforwic	Antwerp	Ribe
Cattle	44.5	52.6	53.6	63.8	37.6	53.1
Sheep/goat	22.9	32.1	22.0	26.3	23.7	20.9
Pigs	32.5	15.3	24.4	10.0	38.1	26.0

Table 2.3 Species ratios based on NISP from Middle Saxon Ipswich compared to the species ratios from a number of contemporary sites in England and on the Continent

could have supplied Ipswich. Archaeological research has shown that large numbers of pigs were being raised in Wicken Bonhunt, Essex and St Albans, Hertfordshire during the Middle Saxon period (Crabtree 2012; Serjeantson *et al*. 2018). Pigs can be driven to market over great distances (see Essig 2015), and Wicken Bonhunt and St Albans are only 67 and 108km from Ipswich as the crow flies and 106 and 138km by car on modern roads. It is also possible that the residents of Ipswich received some of their pork as salted and barrelled meat. Table 2.4 shows the body-part data for the Middle Saxon pigs from both Ipswich and Wicken Bonhunt. While skulls and mandibles are the most commonly represented pig skeletal elements at most Anglo-Saxon and medieval sites in eastern England, the disparity between the number of cranial and post-cranial fragments seen at Wicken Bonhunt and Ipswich is particularly striking. Table 2.5 compares the numbers of pig cranial elements (skull, mandible, and maxilla) and major limb bones (scapula, humerus radius, ulna, innominate, femur, tibia, fibula) at Wicken Bonhunt and Ipswich. At Ipswich, cranial elements make up less than 40% of the major skull and limb bones, while at Wicken Bonhunt they make up over 90%. I have argued elsewhere (Crabtree 2012, 27) that Wicken Bonhunt was a site of specialised pork production. Sites such as Wicken Bonhunt may have helped to provision Ipswich. Future isotopic analyses may shed further light on this issue (see, for example, Hammond and O'Connor 2013). Preliminary strontium isotope data from Haithabu show that 83% of the pig bones tested were derived from non-local sources (Becker and Grupe 2012, 258).

Continental 8th- and 9th-century sites provide some possible parallels for the species ratios seen at Ipswich. Unpublished studies of the faunal remains from Quentovic show that the 8th–9th-century assemblages were dominated by cattle, followed by caprines and a small number of pigs (Yvenic, personal communication). These species ratios are similar to the patterns seen at Eorforwic, Hamwic and Lundenwic. The species from Dorestad are also similar to the other Anglo-Saxon *emporia*. About two-thirds of the large domestic mammals from the hand-collected assemblages are cattle, followed by smaller numbers of caprines and pigs (Prummel 1983, 74–75). At Haithabu, however, pigs were more common than either cattle or caprines, and proportionally more pigs were found in the harbour area than in the settlement itself. Pigs make up 55.2% of the main domestic species from Haithabu harbour and 45.8% from the settlement (Plogmann 2006, 40). Many of the Haithabu cattle and sheep were older individuals, suggesting that they were sent to market after having provided traction, transport and fibres (Becker and Grupe 2013, 256). Cattle were the most commonly recovered domestic mammals from Ribe (53%), followed by smaller numbers of pigs (26%) and caprines (21%) (Hatting 1991, 44). The closest parallel to Ipswich is seen in the species ratios for the 8th- to 10th-century faunal collection from the Burcht site in Antwerp (Figure 2.5). The Antwerp collection shows slightly more pigs than cattle, with relatively small numbers of sheep and goats. At Ipswich, sheep and goats were distinguished primarily on the basis of horn cores. More recent studies of the Antwerp fauna show a sheep-to-goat ratio of about 10 to 1 (Crabtree *et al*.

	Wicken Bonhunt	% Wicken Bonhunt	MS Ipswich	% MS Ipswich
Skull	6405	39.4	347	11.9
Maxilla	1640	10.1	102	3.5
Mandible	2925	18.0	393	13.4
Atlas	35	0.2	4	0.1
Axis	18	0.1	2	0.1
Scapula	342	2.1	259	8.9
Humerus	206	1.3	195	6.7
Radius	126	0.8	177	6.1
Ulna	172	1.1	157	5.4
Carpal	0	0.0	1	0.0
Metacarpus	250	1.5	166	5.7
Innominate	182	1.1	69	2.4
Femur	107	0.7	84	2.9
Tibia	170	1.0	153	5.2
Fibula	135	0.8	44	1.5
Astragalus	10	0.1	51	1.7
Calcaneus	42	0.3	121	4.1
Other Tarsals	0	0.0	8	0.3
Metatarsus	269	1.7	137	4.7
Metapodium	76	0.5	39	1.3
First Phalanx	29	0.2	86	2.9
Second Phalanx	3	0.0	33	1.1
Third Phalanx	8	0.0	10	0.3
Teeth/Fragments	3125	19.2	285	9.8

Table 2.4 Body-part distribution for pigs from Middle Saxon Ipswich and Wicken Bonhunt

Site	N Cranial	% Cranial	N Limb	% Limb
Wicken Bonhunt	10970	90.6	1142	9.4
Ipswich Middle Saxon	752	39.8	1138	60.2

Table 2.5 Comparison of the numbers (NISP) and proportions of cranial and main limb bone elements at Middle Saxon Ipswich and Wicken Bonhunt

2017). The major difference between the Ipswich and Antwerp faunal assemblages is the presence of some possible wild boar in the Antwerp sample. Using the criteria suggested by Evin *et al.* (2014), all of the Ipswich pigs fall clearly within the domestic pig category. At Antwerp, on the other hand, about 20% of the pigs appear to be wild boar based on measurements on the upper and lower third molars.

Turning to the wild mammals, it is clear from Table 2.1 that wild mammals played only a minor role in the Middle Saxon economy at Ipswich. Hunting appears to have played a limited role at the other British *emporia* as well. In an assemblage of nearly 50,000 identified fragments, Bourdillon and Coy (1980, table 17.1) identified only 12 post-cranial bones of red deer and 8 bones of roe deer. An additional 64 fragments of red deer antler appear to have been raw materials for bone-working (Bourdillon and Coy 1980, 82). Although numerous red deer antler fragments were recovered from Anglian York, post-cranial remains of red and roe deer very rare (O'Connor 1991, table 69). O'Connor (1991, 294) concludes that 'Anglian samples were characterised by a very low diversity of taxa... Hunting was unimportant....' The excavations at the London Opera House yielded a small number of red deer and roe deer bones, along with a single bone each of hare and whale. Similar evidence was recovered from the Peabody site where the evidence for hunting was limited to a very few post-cranial remains of red and roe deer (West 1989, 152). These data clearly indicate that hunting played a minimal role in provisioning the Anglo-Saxon *emporia* including Ipswich.

Most of the continental *emporia* also yielded limited evidence for hunting. At Haithabu, wild mammals make up between 1 and 2% of the identified mammal specimens (Becker and Grupe 2012, 256). Wild mammals make up only 0.3–1.3% of the identified faunal remains from Dorestad (Prummel 1983, 74–75). There is also little evidence for hunting at Quentovic (Yvenic, personal communication). At Ribe, there is no clear evidence for mammal hunting. The red deer antler pieces seem to be associated with the manufacture of bone combs (Hatting 1991, 53). There is somewhat more evidence for hunting at the non-*emporium* site of Antwerp. In addition to the evidence for wild boar, the assemblage also yielded the remains of red deer, roe deer, hare, rabbit and beaver. The overall character of the faunal remains from Antwerp is somewhat more rural than what we see at the *emporia*, and this is reflected in the insect remains as well (Crabtree *et al.* 2017).

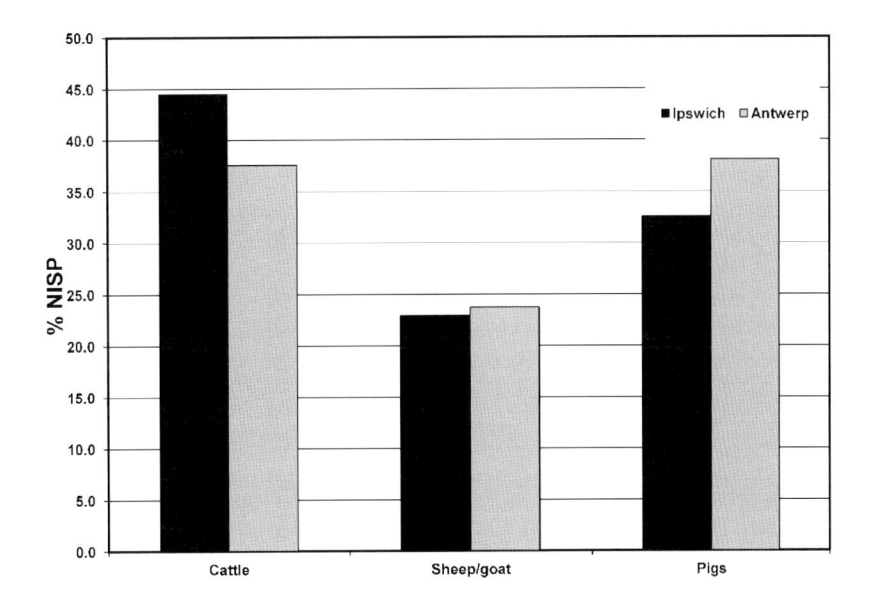

Figure 2.5 Species ratios based on NISP for Middle Saxon Ipswich and 8th–10th-century Antwerp

Substantial numbers of chickens and domestic geese were recovered from Middle Saxon Ipswich (Table 2.1). As noted above, the wild bird assemblage is comparatively depauperate, lacking many of the wild birds including water birds and waders that are typically recovered from Early and Middle Saxon sites in East Anglia (Crabtree 2012, table 3.9). In particular, the excavations at West Stow (Crabtree 1990), West Stow West (Crabtree 2013), Brandon (Crabtree and Campana 2014), and Wicken Bonhunt (Crabtree 2012, table 3.9) all yielded evidence for crane, a bird that was not recovered from Middle Saxon Ipswich. Cranes bred in East Anglia until about 1600 (British Ornithologists' Union 1971; Yalden and Albarella 2008, 82) and are once again breeding in northwest Suffolk (Royal Society for the Protection of Birds 2009). Albarella and Thomas (2002) have noted that while wild birds such as cranes made up a relatively small part of the medieval diet, they may have served as luxury foods. As noted above, many of the wild bird remains recovered from Ipswich were corvids, which are scavengers and are unlikely to have been part of the Middle Saxon diet.

Wild bird remains were also rare at the other British *emporia*, including both the Opera House site (Rielly 2003, table 72) and the Peabody site (West 1989) in London. Only 42 wild bird remains (0.01% of the identified fauna material) were recovered from Hamwic, and many of those birds were scavengers, including gulls and corvids that may have been attracted to the rubbish produced by the Middle Saxon settlement (Bourdillon and Coy 1980, 118). Wild birds were also rare at Eorforwic, and O'Connor (1991, 260) notes that most of these species can be classed as 'scavengers or other species likely to have lived around a site of human occupation.' In short, the zooarchaeological data from Middle Saxon Ipswich and the other Anglo-Saxon *emporia* indicate that fowling played a minimal role in the economy and diet.

The contemporary continental sites provide a more mixed picture. Despite the rich environment for birds in the vicinity of Quentovic, the faunal assemblage from the site provides very limited evidence for fowling (Yvenic, personal communication). Wild birds are also very rare at Dorestad, making up 0.1–0.3% of the identified faunal remains from the hand-collected assemblages (Prummel 1983, 76–77). At Haithabu, on the other hand, a diverse range of wild bird species was recovered. Wild birds make up less than 13–18% of the Haithabu avian assemblages, but a total of 65 different species was recovered and identified from the excavations (Becker and Grupe 2012, 150–151). This level of diversity is not seen at any of the English *emporia*. Anatid species dominate the wild bird assemblage from Haithabu, suggesting that fowling did play a small but important role in provisioning that *emporium*. The 8th-century assemblages from Ribe also produced a fairly long list of wild bird species, providing some evidence for occasional fowling (Hatting 1991, 54–55).

IV. Domestic Animals from Middle Saxon Ipswich

From the above discussion, it is clear that the residents of Ipswich were primarily provisioned with domestic mammals and birds and that hunting and fowling played a very minimal role in the Middle Saxon diet. In this section we will examine the biometric data and age profiles for the domestic species in order to understand the ways that the inhabitants of Ipswich were provisioned with meat and other animal products.

Domestic Mammals

Species ratios based on NISP show that cattle were the most common animals recovered from Middle Saxon Ipswich, and, given their large size, cattle would have provided the bulk of the meat that was consumed at the site. Body-part distributions for the main domestic mammals are shown in Table 2.6. All the body parts are represented, indicating that whole animals were brought into the town, probably on the hoof. The lack of consistent fine screening is also reflected in the body-part distribution. Small elements such as carpals, tarsals and phalanges are poorly represented, especially for the smaller species. For example, 74 cattle tarsal bones (other than the astragalus and calcaneus) were

	Cattle	% Cattle	Caprine	% Caprine	Pig	% Pig	Horse	% Horse
Skull	238	5.7	171	7.9	347	11.9	0	0.0
Horn Core	163	3.9	74	3.4	0	0.0	0	0.0
Maxilla	32	0.8	20	0.9	102	3.5	1	1.6
Maxillary Teeth	86	2.1	30	1.4	39	1.3	4	6.6
Mandible	333	7.9	316	14.6	393	13.4	1	1.6
Mandibular Teeth	360	8.6	174	8.1	188	6.4	5	8.2
Tooth Fragments	12	0.3	0	0.0	58	2.0	0	0.0
Hyoid	6	0.1	1	0.0	0	0.0	0	0.0
Atlas	15	0.4	3	0.1	4	0.1	0	0.0
Axis	6	0.1	5	0.2	2	0.1	0	0.0
Scapula	173	4.1	230	10.7	259	8.9	3	4.9
Humerus	206	4.9	224	10.4	195	6.7	0	0.0
Radius	225	5.4	151	7.0	177	6.1	4	6.6
Ulna	85	2.0	43	2.0	157	5.4	4	6.6
Carpal	78	1.9	3	0.1	1	0.0	0	0.0
Metacarpus	174	4.1	109	5.1	166	5.7	2	3.3
Innominate	91	2.2	82	3.8	69	2.4	1	1.6
Femur	52	1.2	41	1.9	84	2.9	1	1.6
Patella	3	0.1	1	0.0	0	0.0	1	1.6
Tibia	200	4.8	192	8.9	153	5.2	2	3.3
Fibula	0	0.0	0	0.0	44	1.5	0	0.0
Astragalus	191	4.6	35	1.6	51	1.7	4	6.6
Calcaneus	171	4.1	50	2.3	121	4.1	2	3.3
Other Tarsals	74	1.8	5	0.2	8	0.3	2	3.3
Metatarsus	176	4.2	85	3.9	137	4.7	5	8.2
Metapodium	137	3.3	51	2.4	39	1.3	3	4.9
First Phalanx	466	11.1	55	2.5	86	2.9	5	8.2
Second Phalanx	218	5.2	4	0.2	33	1.1	5	8.2
Third Phalanx	224	5.3	3	0.1	10	0.3	6	9.8

Table 2.6 Body-part distribution for cattle, sheep/goats, pigs and horses from Middle Saxon Ipswich

recovered, while only 8 pig tarsals and 5 caprine tarsal bones were identified.

As noted above, cattle were the most important animal species recovered from Middle Saxon Ipswich, and detailed analysis of the age profiles for this species can provide important information on urban provisioning. The data based on epiphyseal fusion are presented in Table 2.7. The data indicate that a very small proportion of the cattle were killed during the first 18 months of life and that only about a quarter of the cattle were killed by the age of three years. About half the cattle survived to more than four years of age. The ageing data based on dental

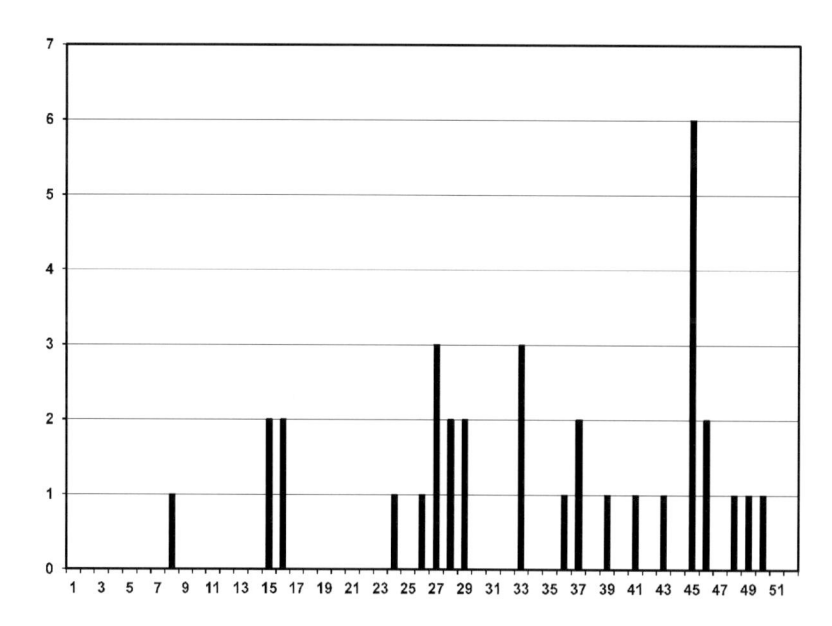

Figure 2.6 Mandible Wear Stages following Grant (1982) for Middle Saxon cattle from Ipswich

	N. Fused	N. Unfused	% Unfused
7–18 months			
D. Scapula	93	3	3
D. Humerus	165	13	7
P. Radius	112	2	2
Total	*370*	*18*	*5*
24–36 months			
D. Metacarpus	82	26	24
D. Tibia	120	44	27
D. Metatarsus	79	28	26
Total	*281*	*98*	*26*
36–42 months			
P. Calcaneus	73	56	43
42–48 months			
P. Humerus	1	2	67
D. Radius	49	37	43
P. Ulna	6	23	79
P. Femur	5	5	50
D. Femur	15	9	38
Total	*76*	*76*	*50*

Table 2.7 Epiphyseal fusion data for Middle Saxon cattle from Ipswich

eruption and wear (Figure 2.6) show a similar pattern. While some younger and market-age cattle were clearly slaughtered and consumed, the assemblage also includes a number of older cattle (Mandible Wear Stage or MWS >36) that were more than 4 years of age. These older cattle may have been sent to market when they were no longer useful for breeding, traction, and dairying, although there is no clear archaeological evidence for traction pathologies in the Middle Saxon faunal assemblage. They were certainly not spavined animals that had spent many years pulling ploughs and carts.

The age profile for the Ipswich Middle Saxon cattle is paralleled by the data from Melbourne Street in Hamwic. At Hamwic, 22% of the cattle were killed at about 2.5 years of age, but nearly half the cattle were adult animals with fully worn dentitions (Bourdillon and Coy 1980, 108). The data from Anglian York also show a non-selective slaughter pattern for cattle (O'Connor 1991, 248–9). The slaughtered cattle include juvenile, immature, subadult, adult, and elderly animals. The oldest animals are probably worn out dairy cattle or plough oxen, but a number of younger, market-age animals was also identified. Adult and elderly cattle mandibles make up the majority of the ageable mandibles recovered from the London Opera House site, but the assemblage also included some juvenile, subadult, and adult animals as well. In general, the cattle age profiles from the Anglo-Saxon *emporia* show a relatively unspecialised pattern of slaughter. All the *emporium* sites yielded substantial numbers of adult or elderly animals, but the assemblages also included young and market-age animals as well. Sexing data can be used to determine whether these adult and elderly animals were excess animals from dairy herds and/or plough teams.

Measurement data have often been used to identify cows, bulls and oxen in the archaeological record, since relatively few cattle bones are unambiguously sexually dimorphic. In terms of overall body proportions, female cattle are relatively small and slight. Since castration delays epiphyseal fusion, the limb bones of castrates (oxen) are generally quite long. Intact bulls are relatively short but stocky. Osteometric data for the Middle Saxon cattle from Ipswich are presented in Table 2.8. The table includes a selection of length and breadth measurements designed to reflect both animal size and robusticity. In addition to the bone measurements (following von den Driesch 1976), withers heights were calculated using Fock's factors for metapodia and Matolcsi's factors for other long bones, following the recommendations of von den Driesch and Boessneck (1974). The intermediate or castrate values were used in the calculation of withers heights for metapodia.

Recent research on late Roman and Early Saxon faunal assemblages has shown that Early Saxon cattle did not maintain the size improvement that was introduced by the Romans (Rizzetto *et al.* 2017). The breadth measurements recorded for Middle Saxon Ipswich are generally quite similar to those seen at Early Saxon West Stow (Crabtree 1990), but the Ipswich long bone measurements include some larger individuals. The average estimates withers height of 116.8 is comparable to the mean wither heights for cattle from Anglian York at 114cm (O'Connor 1991, 270), Middle Saxon Hamwic at 115–116cm (Bourdillon and Coy 1980, 105), and Dorestad at 116cm (Prummel 1983, 171, 178). The cattle from Haithabu, on the other hand, were quite small, with an average estimated withers height of only 109cm (Reichstein and Tiessen 1974, cited in Bourdillon and Coy 1980, 106). Withers height estimates for the cattle from Haithabu harbour are also quite small, ranging from 110.9 based on metacarpi to 111.7 based on the metatarsi (Plogmann 2006, 46).

The difference between the Ipswich Middle Saxon cattle and the West Stow 5th–6th-century cattle can be

Measurement	*Mean*	*Min.*	*Max.*	*S*	*C.V.*	*N*
Radius Bp	73.4	65.1	86.0	4.8	6.5	36
Metacarpus GL	188.9	172.0	207.0	9.1	4.8	37
Metacarpus Bd	56.7	47.8	70.5	5.8	10.2	46
Tibia Bd	57.8	49.5	69.3	4.8	8.3	92
Astragalus GLl	61.5	53.3	72.4	3.9	6.3	108
Metatarsus GL	216.3	204.5	229.7	8.5	3.9	18
Metatarsus Bd	51.5	46.5	62.6	4.1	8.0	42
Withers Height (cm)	116.8	105.4	127.3	5.4	4.6	55

Table 2.8 Osteometric data for Middle Saxon cattle from Ipswich

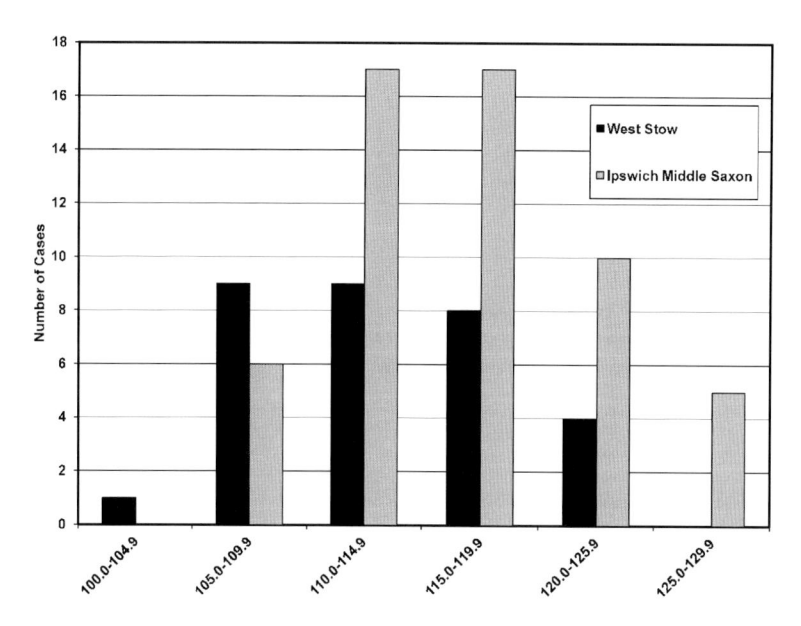

Figure 2.7 Distribution of withers heights for cattle from Early Saxon West Stow and Middle Saxon Ipswich

seen clearly in the distributions of the withers height estimates (Fig. 2.7). The critical question is the following: is there evidence for cattle size increase in the Middle Saxon period, or do these longer limb bone measurements reflect a change in the sex ratios? Were more castrates sent to market in Middle Saxon Ipswich? Metapodial indices (Howard 1963) can be used to distinguish male and female cattle. The metacarpal index is calculated as follows: Bd/GL X 100. Plotting this index against the GL of the metacarpus will generally show a segregation of females and males. These data indicate that most of the complete cattle long bones from West Stow came from female animals (Crabtree 1990, figs 19 and 20). On the other hand, metapodial indices for Middle Saxon cattle from Ipswich indicate that about one-third of those animals were male (Crabtree 2012, fig. 5.8).

A principal components analysis (PCA) was carried out on the complete cattle metapodia from all periods at Ipswich using the following measurements: greatest length (GL), proximal breadth (Bp), minimum diameter of the diaphysis (SD), and distal breadth (Bd) (see Table 2.9). The data were corrected for size, since the GL is always several times larger than the other measurements. A scaled principal component analysis was performed using prcomp in R 3.3.1. Visualisations were performed using the factoextra 1.0.4 package in R. All the variables contribute to the first principal component, which reflects overall size. Both the GL and the SD contribute to the second principal component that reflects bone length in relation to robusticity. The biplot of the first and second principal components is shown in Figure 2.8.

The initial identifications as to sex were determined by visual inspection. The biplot of the sexes is shown in Figure 2.9, and it supports the sex determination based on visual inspection. Although the numbers of completely measureable metacarpi are relatively small, it is clear that the Middle Saxon, Early Late Saxon and Early Medieval assemblages included both cows and oxen. The small Middle Late Saxon assemblage included only 4 cows.

In conclusion, the ageing and measurement data indicate that the inhabitants of Ipswich had access to both market-aged cattle and older cattle that were no longer needed for traction, breeding, and dairying. The ageing evidence closely parallels the age profile for the cattle that were recovered from Anglian York. The York assemblage included both sub-adult cattle aged between 18 months and 3.5 years and older cattle aged between 4 and 9 years (O'Connor 1991, 248–9). The cattle from both Anglian York and Middle Saxon Ipswich clearly represent consumer assemblages. As O'Connor (1991, 249) notes, 'This is not the age distribution one would expect from a site of cattle breeding, but neither can it be readily explained in terms of exploitation concentrating on meat or milk.' The presence of both market-aged animals and older animals that are no longer useful for agro-pastoral purposes points to close links between Middle Saxon Ipswich and the surrounding countryside.

Pigs are the second most important sources of meat for Middle Saxon Ipswich. Unlike cattle and sheep, they do not provide secondary products such as milk, wool, and traction. While European medieval pigs were traditionally raised in woodland areas, pigs can also be reared in urban environments where they can subsist on human refuse, including both rubbish and human waste. The Chinese character for pigs includes the roof of an outhouse.

The ageing data for the Middle Saxon pigs from Ipswich are based on both dental eruption and wear (Fig. 2.10) and epiphyseal fusion of the limb bones (Table 2.10). The data point to the consumption of pigs that were killed throughout the first three years of life, with a small proportion of the animals surviving to more than two and a half to three years of age. The presence of some very young animals (suckling pigs) suggests that at least some of the animals that were consumed in Ipswich were raised in and around the '*wic*'.

The measurements taken on the Middle Saxon pigs from Ipswich are shown in Table 2.11. Withers height estimates were calculated for the few complete limb bones using Teichert's factors, following von den Driesch and Boessneck (1974). These pigs are generally similar in size to the pig remains that were recovered from Hamwic (Bourdillon and Coy 1980, 112) and Brandon (Crabtree 2012, 52–3). As noted above, the lengths of the lower third

Phase	GL	Bp	SD	Bd	Sex
MS	177.0	60.4	34.6	62.8	Bull
MS	172.0	50.3	29.0	51.8	C
MS	192.0	52.7	29.9	54.5	O
MS	178.5	50.2	27.0	52.4	C
MS	193.0	59.4	33.4	62.5	O
MS	191.0	59.5	37.0	65.0	O
MS	187.0	51.8	28.2	52.1	C
MS	193.0	59.6	36.1	62.5	O
MS	181.0	48.9	27.0	50.0	C
MS	177.0	50.1	29.5	54.2	C
MS	184.5	51.0	27.5	51.8	C
MS	202.0	60.1	36.5	65.3	O
MS	184.5	52.9	30.1	54.7	?C
ELS	182.9	52.5	29.6	55.4	?C
ELS	170.4	45.5	25.8	50.0	C
ELS	180.0	52.4	29.9	53.7	C
ELS	199.3	59.1	33.2	62.0	O
ELS	192.6	57.1	32.8	58.1	O
ELS	200.0	65.8	38.2	65.8	O
ELS	186.0	59.6	32.2	52.5	O
ELS	185.0	49.5	28.4	51.0	C
ELS	176.2	48.8	27.0	50.3	C
ELS	192.0	55.0	31.3	56.5	O
ELS	191.7	62.9	40.4	64.9	O
ELS	188.6	58.6	34.5	60.9	O
MLS	178.2	49.5	29.9	52.7	C
MLS	179.3	56.1	34.6	60.0	C
MLS	170.5	48.1	28.7	50.8	C
MLS	178.8	47.1	26.8	50.7	C
MLS	177.0	49.0	28.6	51.8	C
EM	180.0	51.3	26.1	52.6	C
EM	184.5	48.9	26.8	50.6	C
EM	201.9	58.4	33.4	62.7	O
EM	168.0	54.6	36.5	58.1	BULL?
EM	185.0	51.3	27.9	53.0	C
EM	179.5	46.7	26.9	49.9	C
EM	179.5	49.0	27.3	49.0	C
EM	192.5	58.3	32.3	62.3	O
EM	189.0	57.0	32.8	64.4	O
EM	183.0	56.1	33.5	60.2	O
EM	197.0	58.2	31.9	61.1	O
EM	187.5	63.5	37.2	66.2	O
EM	182.0	48.3	27.1	48.5	C

Key: C = Cow, O = Ox

Table 2.9 Measurements taken on complete cattle metacarpi from Middle Saxon, Early Late Saxon, Middle Late Saxon and Early Medieval contexts in Ipswich. The sex column indicates the initial sex determination based on visual inspection

	N. Fused	N. Unfused	% Unfused
12 months			
D. Scapula	122	47	28
D. Humerus	120	0	0
P. Radius	119	21	15
Total	361	68	16
24 months			
D. Metacarpus	40	79	66
D. Tibia	55	66	55
Total	95	145	60
24–30 months			
D. Metatarsus	28	88	76
P. Calcaneus	8	83	91
D. Fibula	0	9	100
Total	36	180	83
36–42 months			
P. Humerus	1	8	89
D. Radius	17	63	79
P. Ulna	16	90	85
P. Femur	0	9	100
D. Femur	2	51	96
P. Tibia	3	23	88
P. Fibula	0	2	100
Total	39	246	86

Table 2.10 Epiphyseal fusion data for pigs from Middle Saxon Ipswich; ages are based on Silver (1969)

Chapter 1 distinctions between sheep and goats were based primarily on horn cores. An earlier study of faunal remains from five sites in Ipswich showed that most of the goat remains from the Middle Saxon period were horn cores. Post-cranial remains from goats were quite rare (Jones and Serjeantson 1983). It seems reasonable to assume that most of the post-cranial remains in the assemblages presented here also represent sheep. At Dorestad, Prummel (1983) demonstrated that most of the goat remains were horn cores and that most of those horn cores were from male animals. She suggested that goat horns, possibly with the skins attached, were brought into Dorestad for industrial purposes.

Recent osteometric studies on sheep from eastern England have shown that the earliest Anglo-Saxon sheep maintained the size improvement that was introduced to Britain by the Romans (Rizzetto et al. 2017). In contrast, Middle Saxon sheep from East Anglia are generally smaller than their Early Saxon counterparts. Detailed statistical studies have shown that the Middle Saxon sheep from Brandon are significantly smaller than their West Stow counterparts (Crabtree 2007), even though the majority of the Brandon sheep appear to have been male. The average estimated withers height for the Middle Saxon sheep from Ipswich is 57.8cm, as compared to 56.6cm for Middle Saxon Brandon and 61.1cm for 6th-century Early Saxon West Stow. It is possible that a new, smaller breed of sheep was introduced to East Anglia during the Middle Saxon period. The Ipswich sheep are smaller than the Middle Saxon sheep from Hamwic that

molars indicate that all the Ipswich pigs were within the domestic range.

Caprines are well represented in the Early and Middle Saxon sites in west Suffolk, but they play a relatively minor role in animal economy of Middle Saxon Ipswich. The measurement data for the Middle Saxon sheep and goats from Ipswich are shown in Table 2.12. As noted in

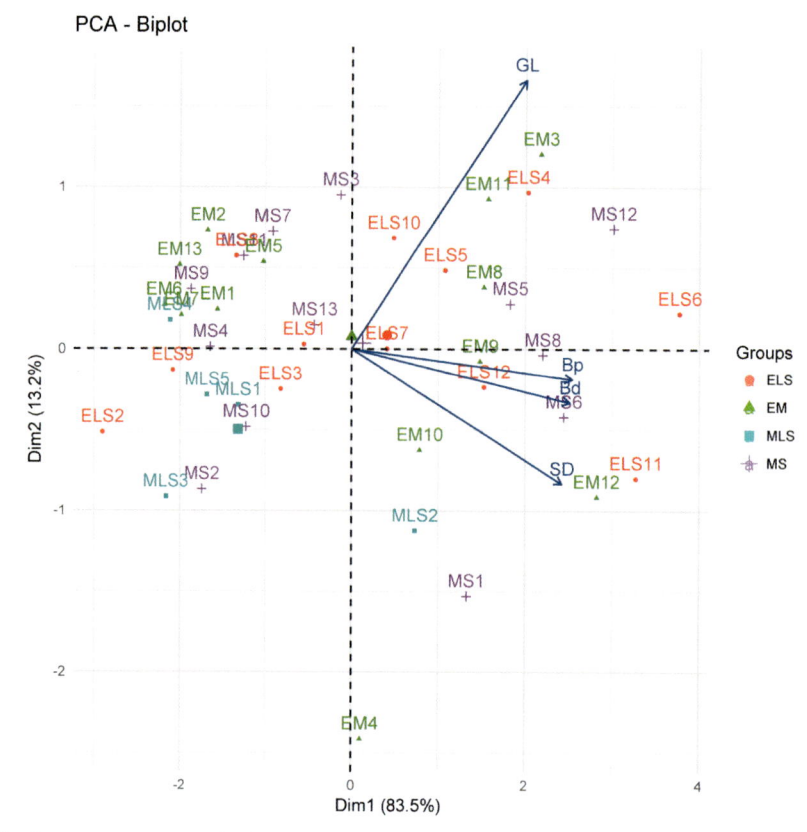

Figure 2.8 Principal components Analysis (PCA) for complete cattle metacarpals from Middle Saxon, Early Late Saxon, Late Saxon and Early Medieval Ipswich. The circled area represents 68% confidence ellipse

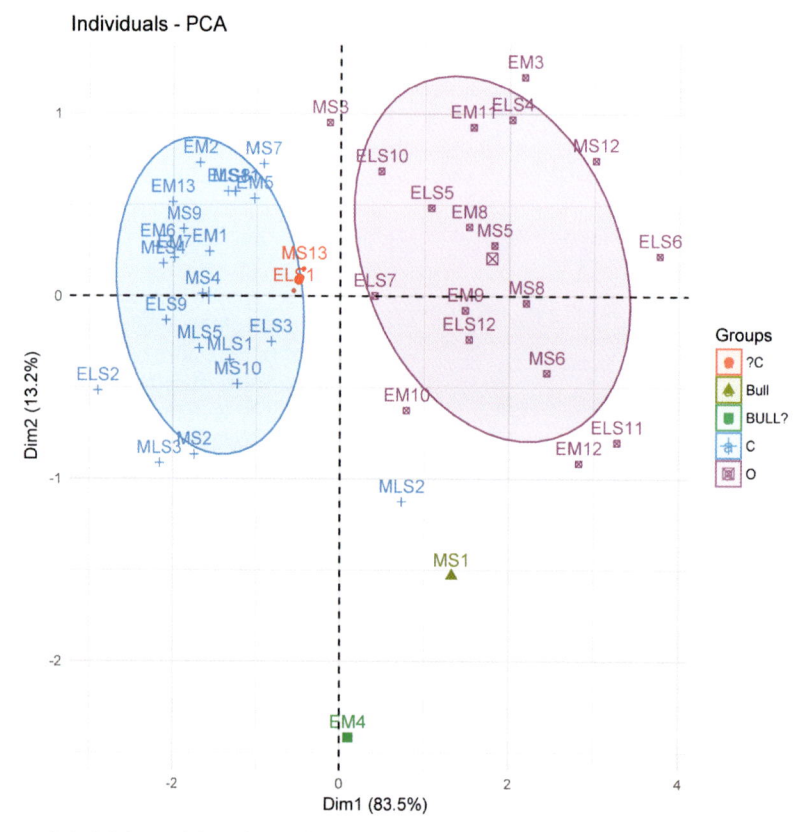

Figure 2.9 Male and female cattle from Saxon and Medieval Ipswich based on PCA

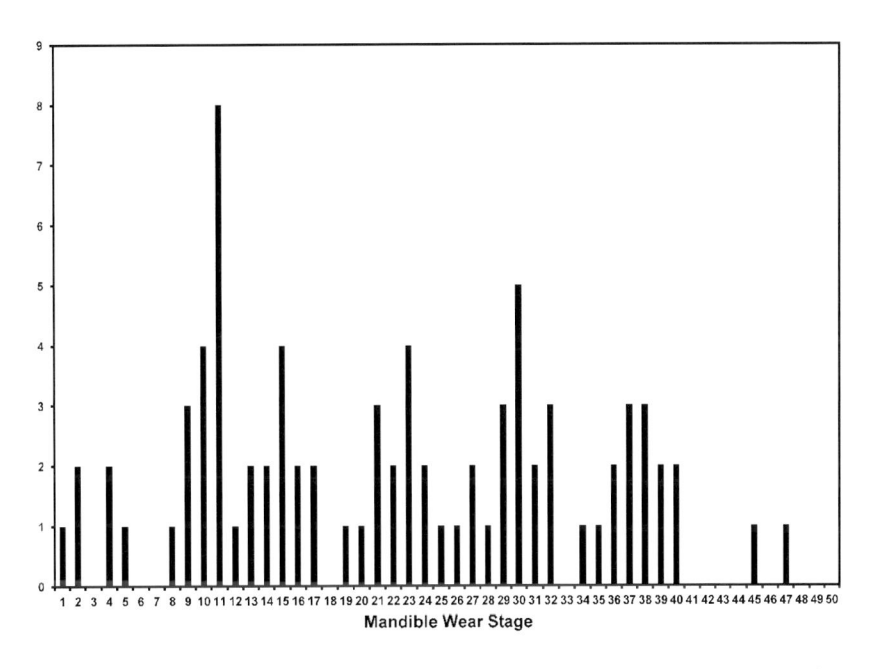

Figure 2.10 Age profile based on dental eruption and wear for Middle Saxon pigs from Ipswich

had an average withers height of 61.4cm, and appreciably smaller than the sheep from Haithabu with an average withers height of 64cm (Bourdillon and Coy 1980, 109). They are also smaller than the sheep from the London Opera House that had an average withers height of 62.8 for Period 4 (AD 675–730) (Rielly 2003, 323, table 97). The sheep from 8th-century Ribe are even larger with an average withers height of 63.5cm based on metacarpals and 66.1 based on metatarsals (Hatting 1991, 49).

Age profiles for the sheep and goats from Ipswich were based primarily on dental eruption and wear (following Grant 1982) since this method allows zooarchaeologists to distinguish adult animals from elderly animals. The distribution of the Mandible Wear Stages for the Middle Saxon caprines from Ipswich is shown in Figure 2.11. The Ipswich Middle Saxon assemblage includes a substantial number of animals that were slaughtered in the second half of the first year of life (broadly equivalent to MWS 7–18). These may represent animals that farmers chose not to overwinter and were culled in the fall of their first year. A relatively small number of animals were culled during the second year of life. The epiphyseal data indicate that relatively few sheep were culled in the first 6–10 months of life, but a more

Measurement	Mean	Min.	Max	S	C.V.	N
Radius Bp	28.1	25.0	31.7	1.6	5.7	67
Tibia Bd	29.0	26.6	32.9	1.5	5.2	31
Astragalus GLl	39.3	34.2	42.0	1.9	4.8	24
Lower M3 Length	31.8	28.3	34.1	1.5	4.8	28
Withers Heights	*GL (mm)*	*WH (cm)*				
Radius	146.2	76.9				
Tibia	176.5	69.2				

Table 2.11 Osteometric data for pigs from Middle Saxon Ipswich

Measurement	Mean	Min.	Max.	S	C.V.	N
Radius GL	142.8	130.8	161.0	8.3	5.8	13
Radius Bp	31.5	28.1	35.8	2.1	6.7	33
Metacarpus GL	118.7	105.4	128.0	8.2	6.9	9
Metacarpus Bd	24.7	23.0	26.9	1.5	5.5	11
Tibia Bd	26.3	22.4	29.7	1.5	5.7	88
Astragalus GLl	27.7	25.7	30.4	1.1	4.0	19
Metatarsus GL	128.0	119.3	139.0	5.7	4.5	14
Metatarsus Bd	24.1	21.5	28.0	1.7	7.1	18
Withers Height (cm)	57.8	51.5	64.7	3.3	5.7	36

Table 2.12 Osteometric data for caprines from Middle Saxon Ipswich

	N. Fused	N. Unfused	% Fused	Age of Fusion
Scapula distal	93	3	97	6–8 mo.
Humerus distal	165	13	93	10 mo.
Radius proximal	112	2	98	10 mo.
Total early fusing	**370**	**18**	**95**	
Tibia distal	120	44	73	1.5–2 yrs
Metacarpus distal	82	26	76	1.5–2 yrs
Metatarsus distal	79	28	74	20–28 mo.
Total middle fusing	**281**	**98**	**74**	
Ulna proximal	6	23	21	2.5 yrs
Femur proximal	5	5	50	2.5–3 yrs
Calcaneus tuber	73	56	57	2.5–3 yrs
Radius distal	49	37	57	3 yrs
Humerus proximal	1	2	33	3–3.5 yrs
Femur distal	15	9	62	3–3.5 yrs
Total late fusing	**149**	**132**	**53**	

Table 2.13 Epiphyseal fusion data for Middle Saxon sheep from Ipswich; ages are based on Silver (1969)

substantial number were culled between 10 months and 1.5 years (Table 2.13). The Ipswich assemblage also includes a large number of market-age animals (2–4 years) and a number of older 4–8 year old animals that may represent off-take from wool herds. No elderly animals were recovered from Ipswich. The pattern is broadly paralleled by the data from Anglian York where the dental ageing data show 'a rather diffuse peak of animals attributable to late first and second year sheep…and another attributed to fully adult sheep of around four to seven years old' (O'Connor 1991, 249). The main difference is that the Ipswich assemblage has more 2–4 year old market-age sheep. The data from the London Opera House are also similar to the Ipswich kill-patterns. Rielly (2003, 321, table 81) shows that the London assemblage included juvenile, immature, sub-adult and adult animals but was lacking any evidence for elderly individuals. The sheep age profile from Hamwic, on the other hand, includes more elderly individuals; 9% of the Hamwic assemblage comes from animals with heavily worn third molars that would have been 8–10 years old when they were slaughtered (Bourdillon and Coy 1980, 110). Most of the sheep from Ribe were slaughtered as adults, and Hatting (1991, 50–51) suggested that this age profile was a reflection of intensive local wool production. The Ipswich assemblage, in contrast, appears to be a bit more consumer-oriented since it includes more young and market-aged animals.

Horse bones are quite rare in the Middle Saxon assemblage from Ipswich, and they are unlikely to have been regular part of the Middle Saxon diet. However, a few butchery marks were apparent on the Middle Saxon horse remains. Splitting of the long bones is a typical Middle Saxon butchery technique (see, for example,

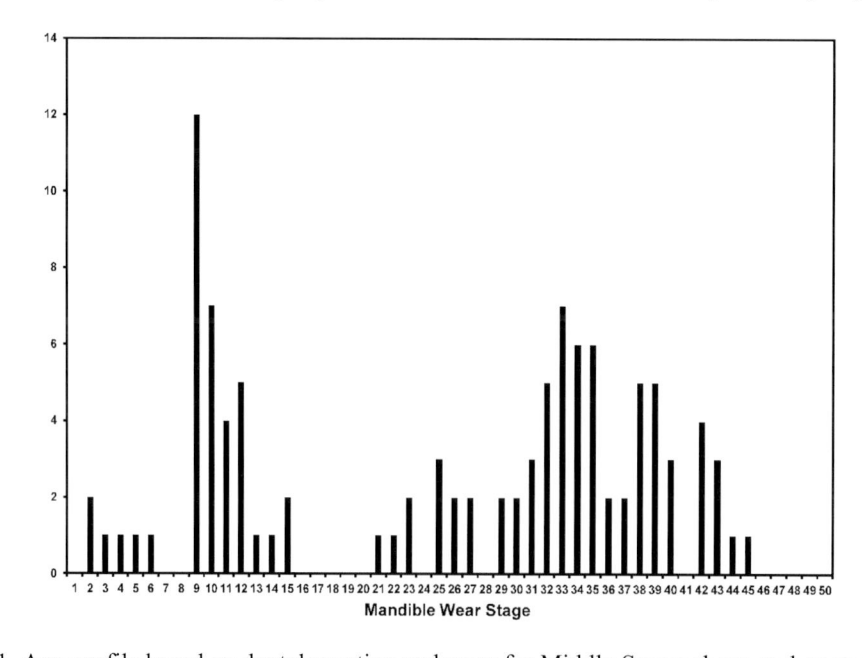

Figure 2.11 Age profile based on dental eruption and wear for Middle Saxon sheep and goats from Ipswich

Crabtree and Campana 2012, 419–20); one horse metapodial and one first phalanx were axially split. In addition, a few chop marks were recorded on horse long bones. This may indicate that horses were an occasional part of the Middle Saxon diet (see Poole 2013 for a full discussion of horse consumption in Anglo-Saxon England). It is also possible that horse bones may have been butchered to feed the meat to dogs.

Measureable horse limb bones were rare in the faunal assemblage. The withers height estimates calculated for four complete horse limb bones are shown in Table 2.14. Withers heights for these horses were calculated using Vitt's factors since lateral lengths (Ll) were not available for the horse bones from Ipswich (von den Driesch and Boessneck 1974). The horse withers heights range from 132 to 139cm or between 13 and 13.3 hands. These horses are actually the size of large ponies. These animals are comparable in size to the horses that were recovered from Hamwic (Bourdillon and Coy 1980, 104) and Ribe (Hatting 1991, 51), although the numbers of horse bones recovered from all these sites are quite small.

Domestic Birds

Nearly all the birds bones recovered from Middle Saxon Ipswich were domestic, and most of them belonged to chickens. The measurements taken on complete chicken long bones are shown in Table 2.15. The Middle Saxon domestic fowl from Brandon showed a distinct bimodality in long bone length (Crabtree and Campana 2014). To determine whether the Middle Saxon chickens from Ipswich exhibited a similar bimodality, the greatest

Element	GL (mm)	WH (cm)
Radius	324.9	134.0
Metacarpus	214.9	133.3
Metatarsus	252.9	132.3
Metatarsus	266.4	139.3

Table 2.14 Withers height estimates for horses from Middle Saxon Ipswich

lengths (GL) of the humerus, ulna, femur, and tibiotarsus were converted to z-scores and plotted on a single graph, as shown in Figure 2.12. The Ipswich chicken limb bones do appear to be bimodally distributed, including a larger number of small fowl and a smaller number of larger chickens. This bimodality is likely to represent sexual dimorphism. The tarsometatarsus is sexually dimorphic in chickens. Male birds usually have spurs, while females do not. These data were not recorded in the initial study of the Ipswich fauna, so I have relied on metrical data for sexing.

V. Provisioning Middle Saxon Ipswich

How did the residents of Ipswich obtain meat and other animal products? Did they purchase their meat at markets where there is direct contact between producers and consumers and buyers and sellers? This is a process that Zeder (1988, 1991) described as direct provisioning. Were they provisioned indirectly through an outside authority and/or food rents (*feorm*)?

Measurement	Mean	Min.	Max.	S	C.V.	N
Humerus GL	68.7	61.6	81.2	5.3	7.7	31
Radius GL	64.1	56.5	71.6	4.1	6.4	11
Ulna GL	67.1	57.4	79.0	6.0	8.9	46
Femur GL	73.6	56.2	84.4	5.9	8.0	30
Tibiotarsus GL	103.5	89.0	117.6	8.8	8.5	108
Tarsometatarsus GL	69.4	56.0	89.2	7.5	10.8	44

Table 2.15 Measurements taken on domestic chicken bones from Middle Saxon Ipswich

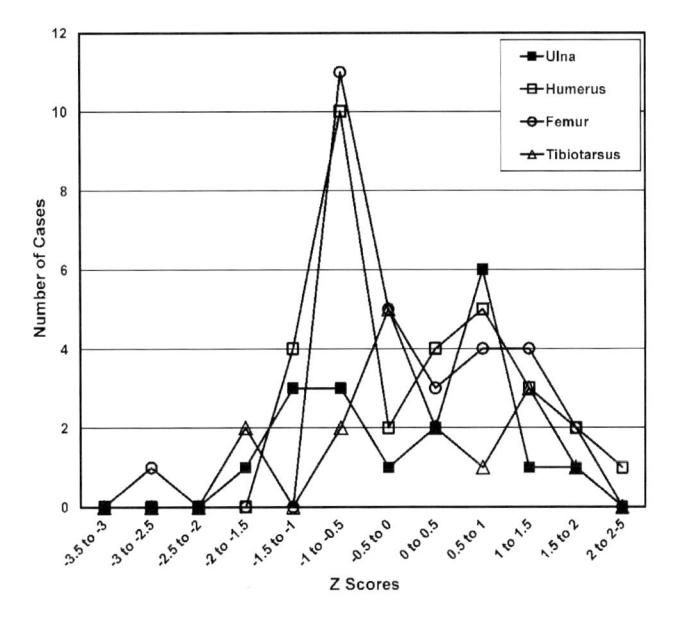

Figure 2.12 Z-scores for chicken limb bones from Middle Saxon Ipswich

Bourdillon (1988, 1994) has argued that the inhabitants of Hamwic were provisioned indirectly, and she has made a convincing case for this proposal. Based on her long-term research at Hamwic, she has suggested that the cattle that were consumed at Melbourne Street were animals that had previously served as traction animals and that the sheep were drawn from herds of wethers that were raised primarily for wool production rather than animals that were raised primarily for food (Bourdillon 1994, 123). She also notes that there were very few foetal, prenatal and neonatal cattle, sheep and pigs recovered from Hamwic, indicating that there was little direct contact between producers and consumers. Bourdillon (1994, 124) suggests that provisioning of Hamwic was orchestrated by some strong central power outside the settlement either as part of a complex of royal properties or through food rents. In support of this model, it is worth noting that Hamwic is also known as Hamtun, suggesting that the site had both a commercial and administrative role (Stoodley 2002, 317). The discovery of a 7th-century high status royal cemetery at St Mary's Stadium has led Stoodley (2002, 326) to suggest that Hamwic began as a royal estate, although there is as yet no clear archaeological evidence for an estate centre. Can this model be applied to Middle Saxon Ipswich?

The situation in Middle Saxon Ipswich differs from Hamwic in several respects. First, Ipswich is not home to a royal estate. Recent archaeological research has located the royal estate at Rendlesham about 20km northeast of Ipswich (see Scull *et al.* 2016). Ipswich, in contrast, seems to be a settlement that was focused on craft production and trade. In addition, the faunal assemblage from Ipswich differs from the Hamwic assemblage in several important ways. Pigs played a much more central role in the Ipswich economy and diet, and they do not provide any secondary products. The mortality profile for the Ipswich pigs includes a few very young animals, also suggesting some more direct contact between producers and consumers and/or the rearing of pigs in and around Ipswich. While the Ipswich assemblage includes substantial numbers of adult cattle and sheep, it also includes a range of younger and market-aged animals as well. As Jones and Serjeantson (1983, 15) conclude in their report on the fauna from five sites in Ipswich, 'the age at death of the cattle, ovicaprids, and pigs suggest that they were slaughtered at optimum age for meat consumption.' The near absence of pathologies on the cattle bones from Middle Saxon Ipswich also suggest that these were not primarily animals that had spent many years of their lives pulling carts and ploughs. The Hamwic assemblage also included a number of very elderly sheep; while these animals were not seen in the Ipswich Middle Saxon faunal assemblage. In summary, the data from Middle Saxon Ipswich point to direct provisioning and to the possibility that the inhabitants of Ipswich obtained their meat through markets.

In the later 20th century, many economic historians thought that markets did not develop in Anglo-Saxon England until the Late Saxon period (see, for example, Jones 1993). Archaeological research that has been conducted in the past 20 years has cast doubt on that assertion. The identification of Middle Saxon coastal trading places and of 'productive sites' points to more extensive trade in the Middle Saxon period. In addition, recent numismatic research (Naismith 2012) has shown that the Middle Saxon economy was partially monetised, and this would have facilitated market exchange. These data would provide some broad support for the idea of meat markets in Middle Saxon Ipswich.

The final argument for direct provisioning of Middle Saxon Ipswich will be presented in greater detail in subsequent chapters. In the following chapters I plan to show that there are long term continuities in urban provisioning at Ipswich from the Middle Saxon through the Early Medieval period.

Chapter 3. Animal Bones from Early Late Saxon Ipswich

I. Introduction

The later 9th century was a period of economic and political change in Anglo-Saxon England. The Viking Great Army invaded England in AD 865, and Ipswich came under Viking control in 880. During the Early Late Saxon period, Ipswich was surrounded by defences for the first time. Archaeological data point to an increase in craft activities at this time, including both copper-alloy and iron metal-working. While Ipswich survived and prospered as a centre of manufacture and trade the fates of the other Middle Saxon *emporia* differed. The occupation of Hamwic ends by 900 at the latest, and by 1000 the entire Hamwic area had reverted to fields. The occupation of the Fishergate region in York continued until about the 870s or 880s when occupation in York moved elsewhere within the town. The Middle Saxon settlement at Lundenwic declined by both size and density in the 9th century, and the Vikings captured the town in 871. The Late Saxon settlement moved downriver to the City of London area. Ipswich is the only one of the major British *emporia* that shows continuity of settlement from the Middle Saxon to the Late Saxon period.

II. The Composition of the Early Late Saxon Faunal Assemblage from Ipswich

The Early Late Saxon features in Ipswich produced a total of 15,535 identified mammal and bird bones and fragments from ten different sites (Table 3.1). Most of these bones were recovered from pit features. The faunal assemblages were dominated by the remains of domestic

Site No.	0802	3410	6202	5202	5901	4201	4801	4601	5203	3104	Total
Species											
Domestic Mammals											
Cattle (*Bos taurus*)	286	105	81	160	318	336	903	518	1405	806	4918
Sheep (*Ovis aries*)	3	2	8	10	3	126	13	34	18	10	227
Goat (*Capra hircus*)	6	0	1	0	2	5	1	8	21	13	57
Sheep/Goat	273	64	98	120	88	1955	450	348	558	658	4612
Pig (*Sus scrofa*)	392	122	81	151	88	339	571	1041	788	884	4457
Horse (*Equus caballus*)	4	2	1	1	3	5	14	7	18	17	72
Dog (*Canis familiaris*)	5	0	2	0	0	16	3	4	22	40	92
Cat (*Felis catus*)	3	0	0	2	4	1	2	8	9	13	42
Wild Mammals											
Red Deer (*Cervus elaphus*)	1	0	5	2	0	66	3	3	0	0	79
Roe Deer (*Capreolus capreolus*)	1	0	0	0	0	1*	3	0	3	0	8
Fox (*Vulpes vulpes*)	0	0	0	0	0	0	0	0	0	2	2
Dog or Fox	0	0	0	0	0	0	0	4	0	0	4
Bat (Chiroptera)	0	0	0	1	0	0	0	0	0	0	1
Whale (Cetacea)	0	0	0	1	0	0	0	0	0	0	1
Domestic Birds											
Chicken (*Gallus gallus*)	60	8	16	20	10	100	230	39	56	159	698
Goose (*Anser anser*)	38	5	3	5	5	9	55	0	27	72	219
Wild Birds											
Mallard (*Anas platyrhynchos*)	0	0	0	7	0	1	0	0	7	0	15
Crane (*Grus grus*)	0	0	0	0	0	0	0	0	1	1	2
Pigeons (*Columba* sp.)	0	0	0	0	0	0	1	0	7	2	10
Finches	0	0	0	0	0	3	0	0	0	0	3
Plovers (Charadriidae)	0	0	0	0	0	2	0	0	0	0	2
Raven (*Corvus corax*)	0	0	0	0	0	0	0	0	0	9	9
Hawks (Accipitridae)	0	0	0	0	0	0	0	0	3	0	3
Falcon (*Falco* sp.)	0	0	0	0	0	0	0	0	0	1	1
Total	1072	308	296	480	521	2965	2249	2014	2943	2687	15535

*This specimen was originally identified as fallow deer

Table 3.1 List of bird and mammal remains recovered from ten Early Late Saxon sites in Ipswich

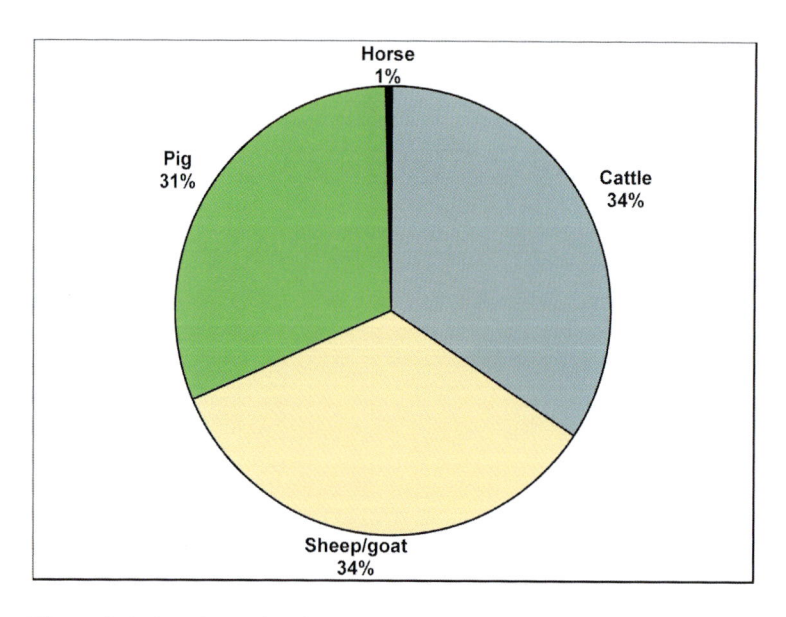

Figure 3.1 Species ratios for Early Late Saxon Ipswich based on NISP

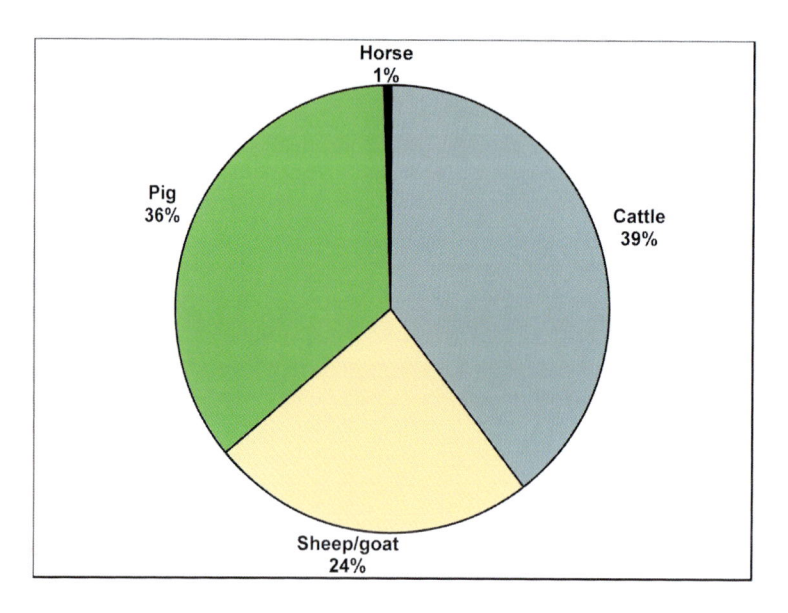

Figure 3.2 Species ratios based on NISP for Early Late Saxon Ipswich (excluding St Nicholas Street 4201)

mammals and birds, and wild species were relatively rare. A single whale bone was recovered from the St Peter's Street site (5202). Cetaceans are rare in medieval sites in eastern England (Gardiner 1997, 189) but small numbers of marine mammal bones have been recovered from other Middle and Late Saxon sites in eastern England including Brandon (Crabtree and Campana 2014) and the Fishergate site in York (O'Connor 1991, 255, table 69). Larger numbers of cetaceans were recovered from the Middle and Late Saxon site of Flixborough in Lincoln (Dobney *et al.* 2007, 48–51) where they were interpreted as a high status food. Ervynck *et al.* (2003, 431) have argued that 'rarities often represent the best examples of luxury foods, simply because they are generally very expensive.' Using that criterion, marine mammals could certainly be seen as luxury foods in Anglo-Saxon sites.

	ELS NISP	*ELS %NISP*	*NISP excl. 4201*	*%NISP excl. 4201*
Cattle	4918	34.3	4582	39.6
Sheep/goat	4896	34.1	2810	24.3
Pig	4457	31.0	4118	35.6
Horse	72	0.5	67	0.6

Table 3.2 Species ratios based on NISP for cattle, sheep/goats, pigs and horses from Early Late Saxon Ipswich including and excluding St Nicholas Street 4201

Both red deer and roe deer were identified from the Early Late Saxon faunal assemblage. Most of the deer remains were antler fragments that were recovered from St Nicholas Street (4201). These remains are antler waste from craft activities. Pat Stevens also identified one radius as fallow deer (*Dama dama*). Sykes (2007) initially argued that fallow deer were a Norman introduction, but her recent research has suggested that they were introduced to Britain around AD 1000 (Sykes *et al.* 2016). Based on the measurements for the St Nicholas Street specimen, it is almost certainly a roe deer rather than a fallow deer. A single fallow deer bone was initially identified in the Late Saxon assemblages from Ipswich that were studied by R.J. Jones (Jones and Serjeantson 1983), but this was subsequently shown to be a misidentification (Sykes 2007, table 13). In short, there is no evidence from Ipswich for a pre-AD 1000 introduction of fallow deer to eastern England. The small numbers of non-antler cervid fragments indicate that deer hunting played a very limited role in the Early Late Saxon economy. The only other non-domestic mammals that were recovered from the Ipswich Early Late Saxon assemblages are a small number of fox bones and a single bone of a bat. Neither the bat nor the foxes are likely to have been part of the Late Saxon diet.

The species ratios for the Early Late Saxon features at Ipswich (Table 3.2 and Figure 3.1) show a substantial increase in the relative importance of caprines when compared to the Middle Saxon assemblages from Ipswich. When the Early Late Saxon faunal collection is considered as a whole, the relative importance of cattle, caprines and pigs is almost equal. This change in species ratios, however, may not reflect a fundamental change in urban provisioning. The assemblage from St Nicholas Street (4201) includes a large number of sheep and goat bones, in addition to the many red deer antler fragments, and it has also yielded some worked bone. These deposits may be specialised deposits (see below). When the faunal remains from St Nicholas Street are removed from the Early Late Saxon totals, the species ratios more closely resemble those of the Middle Saxon period (Figure 3.2). There are no clear cut marks on the many caprine metacarpals and phalanges that were recovered from one pit at the St Nicholas Street site. This is clearly a refuse deposit of some sort, although whether this is the refuse from butchery, skinning, or some other activity is not clear.

The Early Late Saxon faunal remains from Ipswich date to the late 9th century. There are fewer large urban assemblages dating to this period from eastern England than there are from the previous Middle Saxon period. The Coppergate site in York is best known for its well preserved 10th- and 11th-century archaeological remains. While there is also evidence for Roman occupation at the Coppergate site, the area seems to have been abandoned from the 5th through the mid-9th century. The earliest clear post-Roman occupation at Coppergate (Period 3) has been dated to the mid-9th through the late 9th/early 10th century, and it is thus broadly contemporary with the Early Late Saxon remains from Ipswich. The faunal assemblage, however, differs substantially from the contemporary Ipswich material. The Coppergate assemblage includes almost 70% of cattle, followed by smaller numbers of sheep, and only 7% pigs (O'Connor 1989, 151, table 40). Wild animals are rare at Coppergate, and there is no evidence for the kind of bone- and antler-working that is seen at Early Late Saxon Ipswich.

The Early Late Saxon bird remains from Ipswich are dominated by the bones of domestic chickens and geese. The most numerous wild birds are mallard ducks, pigeons and ravens. The avian assemblage from Period 3 at Coppergate, York is also dominated by chickens and geese, with smaller numbers of mallard duck, wood pigeon and raven bones (O'Connor 1989, 194, table 55). The wild bird assemblage from Ipswich also includes two bones of a crane, a single bone of a falcon, and three bones of a hawk. While the numbers are small, the crane bones are likely to represent a luxury food, and the falcon and hawk bones may provide some limited evidence for hawking.

III. Domestic Animals from Early Late Saxon Ipswich

In this section we will examine the osteometric data for domestic mammals and birds and the age profiles for the domestic mammals. The goal of this section is to see if we can identify changes in the patterns of animal use between the Middle Saxon and the Late Saxon periods at Ipswich.

Domestic Mammals

The body-part distributions for the main domestic mammals — cattle, sheep/goat, pig, and horse — are shown in Table 3.3. Two important points can be made about the body-part distribution. First, the small elements such as carpals and tarsals are generally underrepresented, and this is almost certainly a result of hand collection of the fauna. This is true of all the faunal collections from Ipswich. The unique feature of the Early Late Saxon settlement is the large number of caprine metapodia and phalanges recovered from a pit deposit at St Nicholas Street. While caprine metapodia are commonly used in bone-working, these foot bones may also have accompanied hides, since they provide relatively little in the way of meat. There is no clear evidence for butchery or skinning marks on these bones, so the reason for this accumulation is not clear. If a pattern of cooperative diversity existed in late 9th-century Ipswich, butchers might have been located close to hide-, bone- and antler-workers.

Cattle are the most numerous animals recovered from the Early Late Saxon features in Ipswich, and, given their large size, they would have provided the bulk of the meat that was consumed in the town. The measurements taken on the Early Late Saxon cattle bones are shown in Table 3.4. The Early Late Saxon cattle have an average withers height of 114.8; they are slightly smaller on average than the Middle Saxon cattle from Ipswich. These mean data, however, mask a substantial diversity in cattle sizes. The Early Late Saxon withers heights range from 104.1 to 133.3cm, and the distribution of these estimates tails off to the right, indicating a smaller number of very large specimens (Fig. 3.3). The distribution of the distal tibial breadths (Bd) is bimodal for both the Early Late Saxon and Middle Saxon cattle (Fig. 3.4). It seems reasonable to assume that this bimodality reflects sexual dimorphism and that the Middle Saxon and Early Late Saxon assemblages include a large number of cows and a smaller number of males. Nine distal metapodia and phalanges show evidence for exostosis, possibly indicating that

	Cattle	% Cattle	Caprine	% Caprine	Pig	% Pig	Horse	% Horse
Skull	243	6.0	77	1.9	446	12.9	0	0.0
Horn Core	147	3.6	95	2.3	0	0.0	0	0.0
Maxilla	37	0.9	42	1.0	141	4.1	0	0.0
Maxillary Teeth	112	2.7	55	1.3	106	3.1	2	4.1
Mandible	271	6.7	332	8.0	404	11.7	0	0.0
Mandibular Teeth	305	7.5	146	3.5	304	8.8	5	10.2
Tooth Fragments	42	1.0	9	0.2	38	1.1	0	0.0
Hyoid	2	0.0	0	0.0	0	0.0	0	0.0
Atlas	8	0.2	12	0.3	16	0.5	0	0.0
Axis	9	0.2	7	0.2	4	0.1	1	2.0
Scapula	124	3.0	170	4.1	284	8.2	1	2.0
Humerus	217	5.3	216	5.2	236	6.8	1	2.0
Radius	237	5.8	153	3.7	156	4.5	7	14.3
Ulna	85	2.1	62	1.5	172	5.0	4	8.2
Carpal	97	2.4	16	0.4	0	0.0	1	2.0
Metacarpus	164	4.0	411	9.9	181	5.2	2	4.1
Innominate	60	1.5	111	2.7	110	3.2	2	4.1
Femur	57	1.4	67	1.6	107	3.1	1	2.0
Patella	4	0.1	4	0.1	0	0.0	0	0.0
Tibia	216	5.3	191	4.6	160	4.6	5	10.2
Fibula	0	0.0	0	0.0	51	1.5	0	0.0
Astragalus	169	4.1	50	1.2	98	2.8	2	4.1
Calcaneus	196	4.8	71	1.7	57	1.7	1	2.0
Other Tarsals	88	2.2	9	0.2	9	0.3	1	2.0
Metatarsus	176	4.3	445	10.8	177	5.1	5	10.2
Metapodium	120	2.9	39	0.9	42	1.2	3	6.1
First Phalanx	425	10.4	824	19.9	85	2.5	2	4.1
Second Phalanx	241	5.9	222	5.4	44	1.3	1	2.0
Third Phalanx	218	5.4	295	7.1	22	0.6	2	4.1
Sesamoid	4	0.1	1	0.0	0	0.0	0	0.0

Table 3.3 Body-part distributions based on NISP for cattle, sheep/goats, pigs and horses from Early Late Saxon Ipswich

some of these cattle may have been draft animals that were sent to market when they were no longer useful for pulling carts and ploughs. Alternatively, these pathologies may be the result of ageing (see Bartosiewicz *et al.* 1997).

The ageing data based on both epiphyseal fusion of the long bones (Table 3.5) and dental eruption and wear (Fig. 3.5) show that the cattle sent to market in Ipswich include a mixture of market-age cattle and older animals that were no longer needed for breeding, milking and traction. The epiphyseal data indicate that only a small number of cattle were culled in the first year and a half of life. About 60% of the cattle that were sent to market were animals over 42–48 months of age.

Pigs make up over 30% of the faunal assemblage from Early Late Saxon Ipswich. This is one of the most important ways in which Ipswich differs from most other Middle and Late Saxon towns in eastern England. While cattle are nearly always the most common domestic species at Anglo-Saxon towns, sheep are usually second to cattle, as they are at Middle Saxon Hamwic and Phase 3 at the Coppergate site in York. The high proportions of pigs at Ipswich find their closest parallels at continental sites like Antwerp. The reasons for the higher numbers of pigs at Ipswich are not entirely clear. Unlike cattle and sheep, pigs do not provide secondary products, but they are important sources of both meat and fat. If, as I have

Measurement	Mean	Min.	Max.	S	C.V.	N
Radius Bp	76.8	65.1	86.0	4.8	6.5	36
Metacarpus GL	188.9	172.0	207.0	9.1	4.8	47
Metacarpus Bd	56.2	50.0	71.0	5.0	8.9	68
Tibia Bd	57.4	49.2	67.9	4.6	8.1	90
Astragalus GLl	61.5	53.3	72.4	3.9	6.3	108
Metatarsus GL	212.7	191.0	244.5	13.1	6.2	31
Metatarsus Bd	51.6	44.0	60.6	4.6	8.9	77
Withers Height (cm)	114.8	104.1	133.3	5.8	5.1	81

Table 3.4 Measurements taken on cattle bones from Early Late Saxon sites in Ipswich

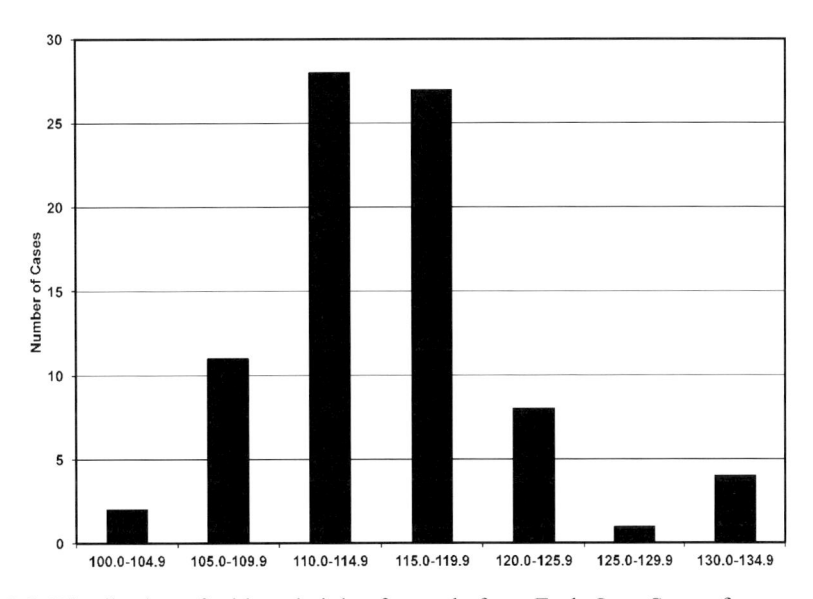

Figure 3.3 Distribution of withers heights for cattle from Early Late Saxon features at Ipswich

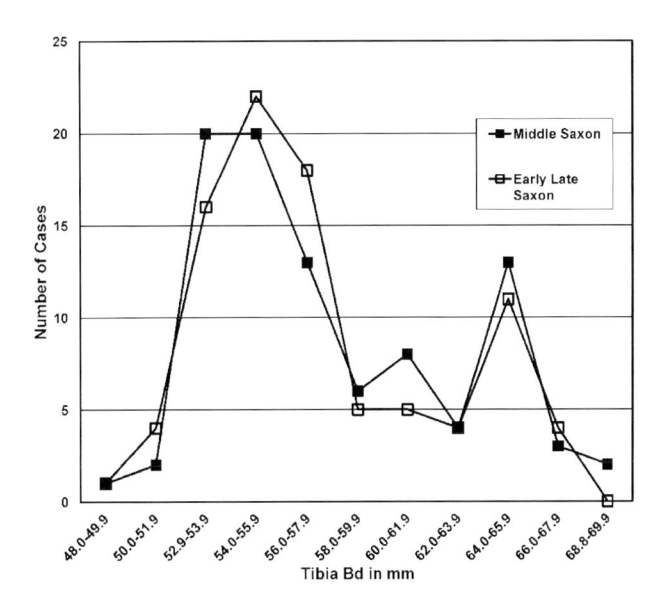

Figure 3.4 Distribution of distal tibial breadths (Bd) for Middle Saxon and Early Late Saxon cattle from Ipswich

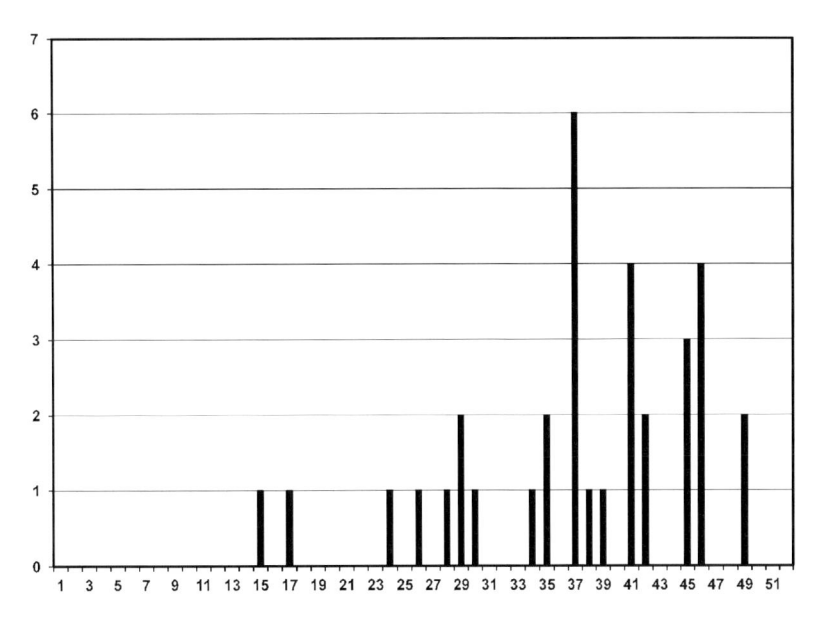

Figure 3.5 Distribution of Mandible Wear Stages for cattle mandibles from Early Late Saxon Ipswich

	N. Fused	N. Unfused	% Unfused
7–18 months			
D. Scapula	79	1	1
D. Humerus	206	22	10
P. Radius	137	4	3
Total	422	27	6
24–36 months			
D. Metacarpus	103	38	24
D. Tibia	152	66	37
D. Metatarsus	116	51	26
Total	371	155	29
36–42 months			
P. Calcaneus	78	83	52
42–48 months			
P. Humerus	6	2	25
D. Radius	88	44	33
P. Ulna	10	25	71
P. Femur	3	2	40
D. Femur	20	15	43
Total	127	88	41

Table 3.5 Ageing data based on epiphyseal fusion for cattle from Early Late Saxon Ipswich; ages are based on Silver (1969)

	N. Fused	N. Unfused	% Unfused
12 months			
D. Scapula	171	51	23
D. Humerus	185	51	22
P. Radius	138	19	12
Total	494	121	20
24 months			
D. Metacarpus	69	163	70
D. Tibia	112	75	40
Total	181	238	57
24–30 months			
D. Metatarsus	44	170	79
P. Calcaneus	9	108	92
D. Fibula	3	9	75
Total	56	287	84
36–42 months			
P. Humerus	1	17	94
D. Radius	3	71	96
P. Ulna	10	124	92
P. Femur	0	11	100
D. Femur	9	85	90
P. Tibia	9	31	78
P. Fibula	0	4	100
Total	32	343	91

Table 3.7 Epiphyseal fusion data for pigs from Early Late Saxon Ipswich; ages are based on Silver (1969)

suggested, the inhabitants of Ipswich were provisioned through a market system, there may have been a higher demand for pork and a lesser demand for cattle and sheep that were raised primarily for other products and sent to market when their productivity declined.

The measurements taken on the pig bones from Early Late Saxon Ipswich are shown in Table 3.6. Three complete pig long bones yielded estimated withers heights based on Teichert's factors (von den Driesch and Boessneck 1974) of just over 70cm. The lengths of the lower third molars are all well within the domestic pig range (Evin *et al.* 2014). This is not unexpected, since there is very little evidence for wild boar from any Anglo-Saxon sites in eastern England.

The age profiles for the Early Late Saxon pigs based on epiphyseal fusion of the long bones are shown in Table 3.7, and the data based on dental eruption and wear are shown in Figure 3.6. Both sets of data point to a fairly continuous slaughter of pigs from young suckling pigs through older pigs with fully worn third molars. There is no clear evidence for seasonal slaughter of the pigs. Instead, the Ipswich pigs appear to have been sent to market throughout the year. Many of the pigs were slaughtered at around 2 to 2.5 years of age. These pigs would have yielded substantial quantities of meat and fat.

With the exception of the concentration of caprine bones in the St Nicholas Street Early Late Saxon deposits, sheep and goats played relatively minor roles in the Ipswich diet and economy during the Saxon and Early Medieval periods. Sheep, however, played a major role in the East Anglian economy throughout the medieval period, and they are the numerically predominant species at rural Anglo-Saxon sites, including West Stow (Crabtree 1990), Brandon (Crabtree and Campana 2014), and West Stow West (Crabtree 2013, Crabtree and Campana 2015).

Measurement	Mean	Min.	Max	S	C.V.	N
Radius Bp	27.6	24.3	31.8	1.6	5.8	77
Tibia Bd	28.6	25.1	33.4	1.7	5.9	62
Astragalus GLl	38.3	32.8	43.3	2.2	5.7	49
Lower M3 Length	31.2	26.3	35.7	2.1	6.7	45
Withers Heights	*GL (mm)*	*WH (cm)*				
Radius	137.1	73.1				
Tibia	181.0	71.0				
Tibia	183	71.7				

Table 3.6 Measurements taken on pig bones from Early Late Saxon Ipswich

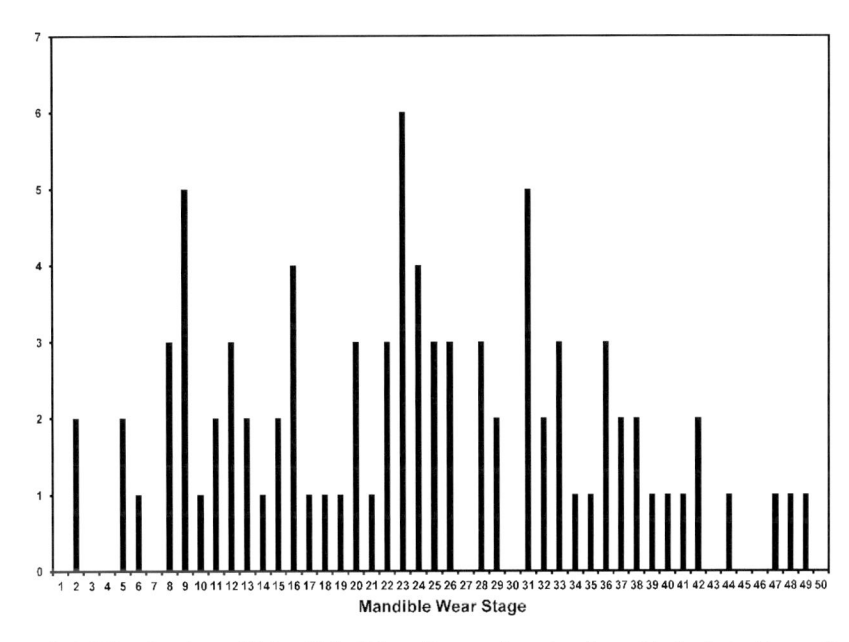

Figure 3.6 Distribution of Mandible Wear Stages for pigs from Early Late Saxon Ipswich

Analysis of the caprine remains from Ipswich can shed light on the relationship between urban consumers.

Measurement data for the Early Late Saxon sheep from Ipswich are shown in Table 3.8. The Early Late Saxon sheep from Ipswich appear to be somewhat larger than their Middle Saxon counterparts, and this can be seen most clearly in the long bone lengths and the withers heights that are calculated from them (Fig. 3.7). A series of Student's t-tests were used to determine whether there were significant size differences between the Middle Saxon and Early Late Saxon sheep from Ipswich. The more conservative 2-tailed t-test was used in all cases. The differences between four of the measurements (Radius Bp, Metacarpus GL, Tibia Bd, and Metatarsus Bd) were non-significant. The differences between the Middle Saxon and Early Late Saxon Radius GL, Metacarpus Bd, and Astragalus GLl were significant at the $p = .05$ level, and the differences between the Metatarsus GL and the estimated withers heights were significant at the $p = .01$ level. In all cases, the Middle Saxon sheep were smaller than their Early Late Saxon counterparts. The larger Early Late Saxon sheep may represent wethers (castrated males) that were sent to market when they were no longer needed for wool production.

The small size of the Middle Saxon sheep from Ipswich is not an isolated phenomenon. For example, the Middle Saxon sheep from Brandon are significantly smaller than their Early Saxon counterparts from West Stow (Crabtree 2007). The average estimated withers height for the Ipswich sheep is 57.8cm, as compared to 56.6cm for Middle Saxon Brandon and 61.9cm for 6th-century Early Saxon West Stow. Recent research has shown that the Early Saxon sheep from eastern England retained the size improvement that was introduced by the Romans (Rizzetto et al. 2017). This does not appear to be the case for the Middle Saxon sheep from East Anglia. The Late Saxon sheep from Ipswich, however, seem to have returned to their larger, Early Saxon size.

The ageing data for sheep and goats from Early Late Saxon Ipswich also yielded interesting results. The age profile for the Early Late Saxon sheep and goats (Fig. 3.8) was based on dental eruption and wear following Grant (1982). In Figure 3.9, these data have been grouped into age classes following Bourdillon and Coy (1980) and compared to the age profile for the Early Saxon site of West Stow (Crabtree 1990, 92, table 46). The age profile for West Stow includes more first-year culls (Stages 1 and 2). These probably represent animals that the Early Saxon farmers chose not to overwinter. The Early Late Saxon assemblage from Ipswich, on the other hand, includes a higher proportion of market-age animals in the 2–4 year age group (Stage 4), and no elderly sheep in the 8–10 year age range were recovered from Early Late Saxon Ipswich. The Ipswich kill-pattern was compared to the mortality

Measurement	Mean	Min.	Max.	S	C.V.	N
Radius GL	148.8	135.6	159.0	6.5	4.5	30
Radius Bp	31.3	26.4	35.5	2.0	6.4	61
Metacarpus GL	123.3	110.0	136.3	5.8	4.7	69
Metacarpus Bd	25.7	22.7	32.4	1.2	4.7	211
Tibia Bd	26.2	22.8	29.4	1.4	5.3	130
Astragalus GLl	28.6	25.8	31.1	1.3	4.5	43
Metatarsus GL	133.3	116.7	147.0	6.8	5.1	68
Metatarsus Bd	24.2	21.9	27.4	1.0	4.1	208
Withers Height (cm)	60.3	53.0	68.3	3.1	5.1	159

Table 3.8 Measurements on Early Late Saxon sheep from Ipswich

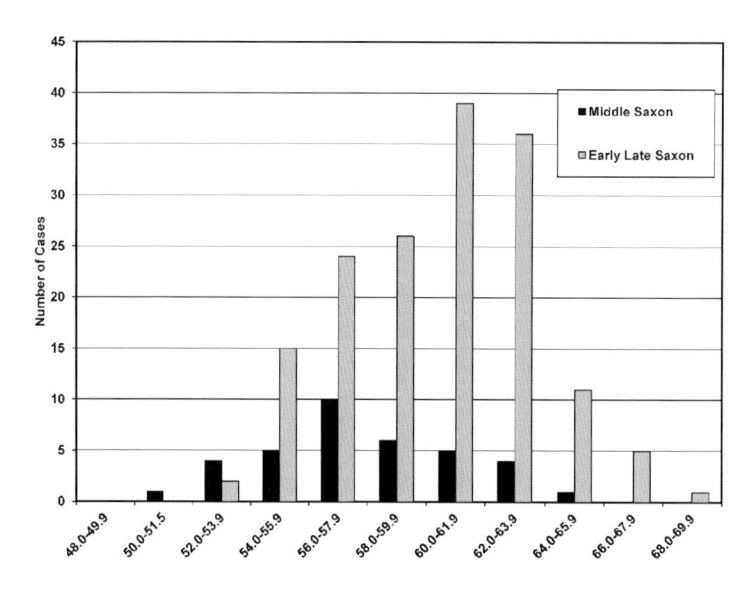

Figure 3.7 Distribution of withers heights for sheep from Middle Saxon and Early Late Saxon Ipswich

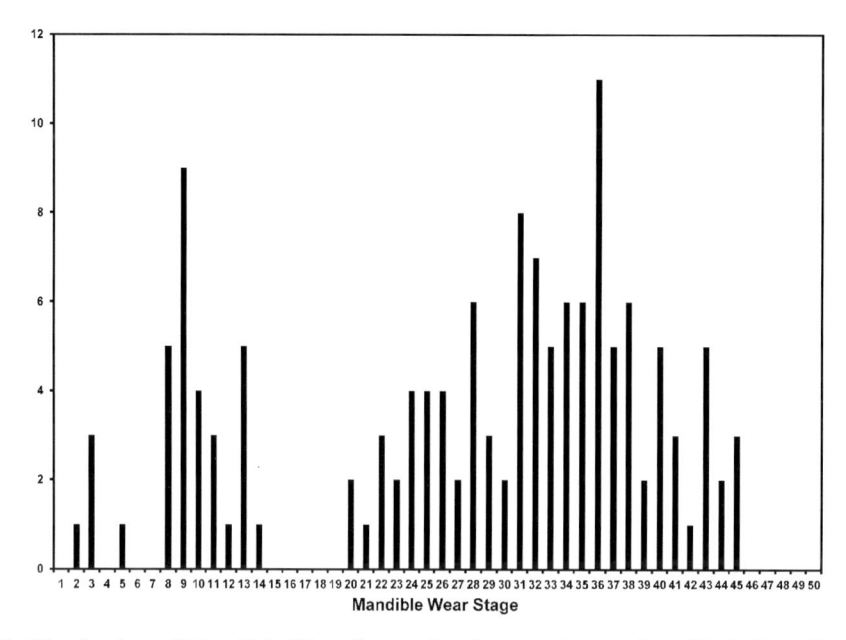

Figure 3.8 Distribution of Mandible Wear Stages for sheep and goats from Early Late Saxon Ipswich

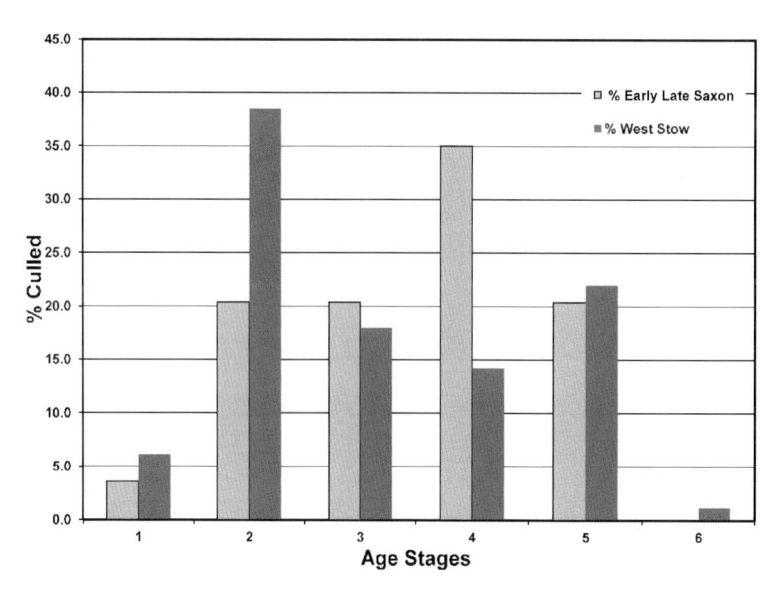

Figure 3.9 Distribution of mandible wear classes for sheep and goats from Early Late Saxon Ipswich compared to the mandible wear data from Early Saxon West Stow

	N. Fused	N. Unfused	% Fused	Age of Fusion
Scapula distal	132	21	14	6–8 mo.
Humerus distal	272	25	8	10 mo.
Radius proximal	137	7	5	10 mo.
Total early fusing	**541**	**53**	**9**	
Tibia distal	180	30	14	1.5–2 yrs
Metacarpus distal	274	30	10	1.5–2 yrs
Metatarsus distal	258	24	8	20–28 mo.
Total middle fusing	**712**	**84**	**12**	
Ulna proximal	15	21	58	2.5 yrs
Femur proximal	7	5	42	2.5–3 yrs
Calcaneus tuber	57	46	45	2.5–3 yrs
Radius distal	74	20	21	3 yrs
Humerus proximal	6	12	67	3–3.5 yrs
Femur distal	17	43	72	3–3.5 yrs
Total late fusing	**176**	**147**	**46**	

Table 3.9 Epiphyseal fusion data for Early Late Saxon sheep from Ipswich; ages are based on Silver (1969)

profile from Early Saxon West Stow using a Kolmogorov-Smirnov test, and the results were significant (D = 0.8333; p = .01). The epiphyseal data for the Early Late Saxon sheep (Table 3.9) suggest that few animals were culled in the first two years of life, but about 30% of the animals were culled between 2 and 3.5 years of age. About half the sheep survived to more than 3.5 years of age. While the epiphyseal data include fewer younger animals, both the epiphyseal and the tooth wear data indicate that a substantial number of the sheep that were consumed at Ipswich were market-aged animals between 2 and 4 years of age. The smaller number of very young caprines based on epiphyseal data may reflect a taphonomic bias against the survival of very young animals with unfused epiphyses. Nevertheless, the Ipswich assemblage appears to be a consumer assemblage that is focused on prime-age meat animals, along with some older animals that may initially have been kept for wool, milk, or breeding.

The complete horse long bones recovered from the Early Late Saxon features at Ipswich, along with the withers heights calculated using Vitt's factors (von den Driesch and Boessneck 1974), are shown in Table 3.10. The withers heights range from 128 to 141cm or between 12.2 and 14 hands. These are large ponies rather than true horses, and they are similar in size to the horse remains recovered from the Middle Saxon features. There is no clear evidence for horse butchery from the Early Late Saxon assemblage.

One of the most interesting features of the Early Late Saxon faunal remains from Ipswich is the presence of a number of complete dog limb bones (Table 3.11). The withers heights for these dog bones were calculated using Koudelka's factors, following von den Driesch and Boessneck (1974). Several of these bones came from a single small dog which had a withers height of about 30cm. This dog would have been similar in height to a Cavalier King Charles spaniel, but it should be noted that modern dog breeds were developed in the 19th century. What is interesting here is that this dog is much smaller than the dogs that have been recovered from rural Early

Element	GL (mm)	WH (cm)
Radius	309.9	128.0
Metacarpus	214.4	132.8
Tibia	351.9	138.8
Tibia	344.4	136.0
Metatarsus	270.4	141.3
Metatarsus	261.9	137.1

Table 3.10 Measurements and withers height estimates for horses from Early Late Saxon Ipswich

and Middle Saxon sites in East Anglia. The dogs from Brandon and West Stow were larger, straight-limbed dogs with withers heights of about 60cm, roughly the size of a modern Alsatian or German shepherd. Small lap dogs were common in Britain during the Roman period (Baxter 2010), but they seem to have disappeared from Anglo-Saxon rural sites in post-Roman times. It is interesting that smaller dogs reappear in urban sites in the later Anglo-Saxon period. The Early Late Saxon faunal assemblage from Ipswich also includes some larger dogs with withers heights of around 50cm.

Element	GL (mm)	WH (cm)
Humerus	140.9	47.5
Humerus*	98.6	33.2
Radius	165.4	53.3
Radius	175.4	56.5
Radius*	87.9	28.3
Ulna*	105.7	28.2
Femur*	106.7	32.1
Tibia*	96.4	28.1

* These specimens are from the same individual

Table 3.11 Measurements and withers height estimates for dogs from Early Late Saxon Ipswich

Measurement	Mean	Min.	Max.	S	C.V.	N
Humerus GL	67.0	60.1	75.2	4.7	7.1	51
Radius GL	63.7	55.9	68.7	4.4	6.8	14
Ulna GL	66.9	57.7	79.0	5.8	8.2	68
Femur GL	75.3	61.8	90.6	6.3	8.3	35
Tibiotarsus GL	106.0	91.4	128.3	9.6	9.1	110
Tarsometatarsus GL	69.4	56.5	81.2	8.0	11.4	21

Table 3.12 Measurements taken on domestic chicken bones from Early Late Saxon Ipswich

Other Late Saxon sites in Britain show a similar diversity in the sizes of the dogs that were kept in the towns. The dog bones from the Coppergate site in York also provide evidence for dogs of different sizes. Most of the dogs appear to be 50–60cm at the withers, but there are also some smaller terrier-sized dogs as well (O'Connor 1989, 186). Bourdillon (2009, 78) notes that the faunal assemblages from the Winchester suburbs also produced the remains of dogs of varying sizes. While most of the Winchester dogs were medium-sized, the Late Saxon features also included some small dogs, including one with a withers height of only 30cm. A diversity of dogs was also recovered from Late Saxon Thetford. Jones (1984, 190) describes a male dog with a withers height of about 54cm that received blows around his muzzle. Additional complete long bones came from a dog with a similar withers height (53cm), and a small dog with curved limb bones and an estimated withers height of only 25cm. Very small lap dogs, like those known from the Roman period, do not reappear until the 16th century (Terry O'Connor, personal communication). See Crabtree (2015b) for a more complete discussion of Anglo-Saxon dog remains.

Domestic Birds

Domestic chickens outnumber domestic geese in the Early Late Saxon deposits from Ipswich by a factor of nearly 3.5 to 1. The measurements taken on the Early Late Saxon chicken bones are shown in Table 3.12. These birds are similar in size to the chicken remains that were recovered from the Middle Saxon features in Ipswich.

IV. Provisioning Early Late Saxon Ipswich

The Early Late Saxon animal bone remains from Ipswich date to the late 9th century. This was a period of political turmoil in eastern England with the arrival of the Great Heathen (Viking) Army in 865. This followed a series of Viking raids that began in the late 8th century. Archaeological data from both Hamwic and Lundenwic indicate that both these *emporia* were in decline by the mid-to-late 9th century. This, however, does not appear to be the case for Ipswich.

Archaeozoological data point to broad continuities in urban provisioning between the Middle Saxon and the Early Late Saxon period in Ipswich. If we exclude the large number of caprine remains that were recovered from the St Nicholas Street site, the overall species ratios are similar between the two periods. Cattle are the most common domestic species, following by pigs, and caprines played a relatively small role in the diet. While horses may have played a very minor role in the Middle Saxon diet, they do not appear to have been part of the Early Late Saxon diet. Hunting played a minor role in the Ipswich economy during both the Middle Saxon and the Early Late Saxon periods. Chickens are more common than domestic geese, and only a few bones of wild fowl were recovered. The inhabitants of Ipswich appear to have access to market-aged cattle, pigs, and sheep, in addition to some older animals that may have been sent to market when their working and breeding lives were over. These data would seem to suggest that the inhabitants of Ipswich obtained their meat through markets.

There are one or two individual finds that suggest that some of Ipswich's inhabitants may have had access to high-status resources. A single whale bone was recovered from St Peter's Street (5202), and a single bone of a falcon, along with three hawk bones, may provide some limited evidence for falconry.

There is at least one difference between the Middle Saxon and Early Late Saxon faunal assemblages that deserves further research. Statistical comparisons of sheep measurements suggest that the Early Late Saxon sheep were significantly larger than their Middle Saxon counterparts. The differences are seen most clearly in limb bone lengths. These data suggest that sheep husbandry had a complex history in East Anglia. As noted above, recent research indicates that the earliest Anglo-Saxon sheep in eastern England maintained the size improvement that was introduced to Britain by the Romans (Rizzetto *et al.* 2017). The Middle Saxon sheep from Ipswich and from rural sites like Brandon appear to be smaller than the Early Saxon sheep from sites such as West Stow. The data from Ipswich suggest that were was some size improvement in the Late Saxon period. Detailed measurement studies from other large Late Saxon sites are needed to confirm this observation. In addition, the publication of original data, rather than just ranges, is most useful for intersite comparisons (see Holmes 2014). The ways in which the Ipswich data were initially recorded make it challenging to publish the original data, but data that have been recorded using modern methods, e.g., West Stow West, can be published and made available to other researchers.

Chapter 4. Animal Bones from Middle Late Saxon Ipswich

I. Introduction

The Middle Late Saxon period in Ipswich is dated to the 10th century. Ipswich returned to Anglo-Saxon control in 920, after being under Viking control during the late 9th and early 10th century. While Ipswich did not expand much during this period, it remained one of the ten largest towns in Anglo-Saxon England. The 10th century is an interesting period for the development of towns in eastern England. While the *emporia* set the stage for the development of urbanism in the 8th and 9th centuries, there is substantial evidence for the development of towns during the 10th century in areas that were under both Viking and Saxon control.

One of the best documented 10th-century towns in eastern England is York where large-scale open-area excavations took place at the Coppergate site (Hall 1984; 1994; 2014). During Periods 4A and 4B (late 9th/early 10th century to *c.* 975), boundaries were laid out, and post-and-wattle tenement buildings were constructed. The excavations revealed evidence for iron-working and other crafts on a commercial scale (O'Connor 1989, table 38). The 10th-century faunal materials from York provide one of the best comparanda for the animal bone remains from the Middle Late Saxon deposits from Ipswich.

The large-scale excavations that were carried out in Winchester between 1961 and 1971 have also documented substantial urban development during the late 9th/early 10th century. Biddle (1990) has shown that Winchester was substantially re-planned at this time, and excavations at the Brook Street site (Biddle 1975) yielded important evidence for both the Anglo-Saxon settlement plan and the craft activities that were carried out there. The site also yielded substantial quantities of animal bone remains. It has also been suggested that the re-planning of Winchester may have served as a model for the

Site No.	1804	0802	3410	6202	5901	6904	4201	4801	4601	5203	3104	Total
Species												
Domestic Mammals												
Cattle (*Bos taurus*)	33	54	47	21	108	49	133	398	133	175	1588	2739
Sheep (*Ovis aries*)	0	1	0	0	3	0	2	5	8	8	29	56
Goat (*Capra hircus*)	0	0	0	0	1	0	42	0	4	1	8	56
Sheep/Goat	35	28	35	5	104	36	246	88	70	137	924	1708
Pig (*Sus scrofa*)	26	47	53	24	88	49	228	99	55	167	1184	2020
Horse (*Equus caballus*)	3	0	1	0	2	0	4	2	1	4	13	30
Dog (*Canis familiaris*)	0	0	1	2	0	0	19	1	1	0	27	51
Cat (*Felis catus*)	0	0	0	0	0	1	0	1	23	2	19	46
Wild Mammals												
Red Deer (*Cervus elaphus*)	0	0	0	0	11	0	1	1	0	0	3	16
Roe Deer (*Capreolus capreolus*)	1	0	0	0	0	0	0	0	0	0	5	6
Hare (*Lepus* sp.)	0	0	1	0	0	0	0	0	3	0	6	10
Rabbit (*Oryctolagus cunniculus*)	0	0	0	0	0	0	0	0	1	0	0	1
Domestic Birds												
Chicken (*Gallus gallus*)	19	2	9	9	0	1	33	13	0	43	552	681
Goose (*Anser anser*)	0	1	3	0	1	0	11	1	0	3	31	51
Wild Birds												
Mallard (*Anas platyrhynchos*)	0	1	4	0	0	0	0	0	0	1	1	7
Swan (*Cygnus olor*)	0	0	0	0	0	0	0	0	0	1	0	1
Crane (*Grus grus*)	0	0	0	0	0	0	1	0	0	0	0	1
Pigeons (*Columba* sp.)	0	0	0	0	0	0	1	0	0	0	2	3
Raven (*Corvus corax*)	0	0	0	0	0	0	0	0	0	0	2	2
Crows (Corvidae)	0	0	0	0	0	0	0	0	0	0	1	1
Common buzzard (*Buteo buteo*)	0	0	0	0	0	0	0	0	1	0	0	1
Hawks (Accipitridae)	0	0	0	0	0	0	0	0	0	0	1	1
Peregrine falcon (*Falco peregrinus*)	0	0	5	0	0	0	0	0	0	0	0	5
Hen harrier (*Circus cyaneus*)	0	0	3	0	0	0	0	0	0	0	0	3
Total	117	134	162	61	318	136	721	609	300	542	4396	7496

Table 4.1 List of bird and mammal remains recovered from Middle Late Saxon Ipswich

development of other Late Saxon towns in Wessex (Biddle and Hill 1971). Unfortunately, the planned volumes on *The Brooks and Other Town Sites in Medieval Winchester* and *The Animals of Early Winchester* are still in preparation more than 45 years after the Winchester excavations were completed in 1971 when I served as a volunteer on the Brook Street site. There are, however, a number of smaller studies of the animal bones from suburban Winchester that have been published (Coy 2009; Bourdillon 2009), and these data can serve as comparanda for the Middle Late Saxon material from Ipswich. Other comparanda include animal bone material from Late Saxon Thetford (Jones 1984) and Flaxengate, Lincoln (O'Connor 1982).

II. The Composition of the Middle Late Saxon Faunal Assemblage from Ipswich

Eleven sites in Ipswich yielded faunal remains that could be dated to the Middle Late Saxon period. Most of this material came from pits, but the faunal remains from the Shire Hall site (6904) were recovered from a ditch. The faunal remains recovered from the Middle Late Saxon features are shown in Table 4.1. The Middle Late Saxon assemblages are dominated by the remains of domestic mammals, primarily cattle, pigs and caprines. Wild mammal remains are rare and include small numbers of red deer, roe deer and hare bones. The single rabbit bone may be intrusive. Sykes (2007) has argued that rabbits were Norman introductions to Britain, but more recent research suggests that they were initially introduced around AD 1000 (Sykes *et al.* 2019).

The bird remains are primarily domestic chickens; relatively few domestic goose bones were recovered from the Middle Late Saxon assemblages. Just over 93% of the domestic bird remains are chicken bones. These data indicate that the importance of domestic chickens increased throughout the Middle and Late Saxon periods at Ipswich.

The bird remains include ravens and crows, wild birds that prosper in urban environments. The most interesting avian remains are the five bones of a peregrine falcon

Measurement (mm)	*Ipswich*	*Female mean*	*Male mean*
Tibiotarsus (GL)	4918	34.3	4582
Tarsometatarsus (GL)	4896	34.1	2810

Table 4.2 Measurements taken on the Ipswich peregrine falcon compared to those for male and female peregrine falcons (Solti 1985)

(*Falco peregrinus*) that were recovered from the Tacket Street site (3410). The bones appear to be the remains of a single individual. Based on the measurements of the tibiotarsus and tarsometatarsus, the Ipswich individual appears to be a male (Table 4.2). Female peregrines, which are larger than their male counterparts, were generally preferred for falconry.

The species ratios for the main domestic mammals — cattle, sheep/goat, pig, and horse — are shown in Table 4.3 and Figure 4.1. The ratios were based on NISP, following Lyman (2008). Cattle are the most common species, as they are in nearly all urban medieval sites in Britain; pigs are second, followed closely by caprines. Only a few horse bones were recovered from the Middle Late Saxon features, and there is no evidence that they formed part of the diet.

Species ratios based on cattle, sheep/goat, and pig only were calculated to make the Ipswich data comparable to other Late Saxon sites in eastern England (Table 4.4). The unique feature of the Ipswich assemblage is that pigs are second in number to cattle. In all other cases, caprines are second in number, although there is a greater emphasis on

	NISP	*%NISP*
Cattle	2739	41.4
Sheep/goat	1820	27.5
Pig	2020	30.6
Horse	30	0.5

Table 4.3 Species ratios based on NISP for cattle, sheep/goat, pig and horse from Middle Late Saxon Ipswich

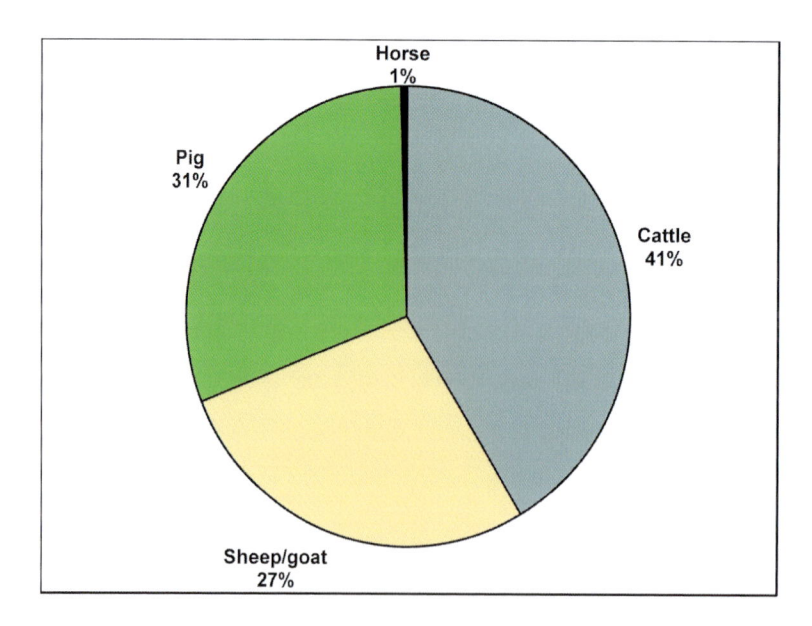

Figure 4.1 Species ratios based on NISP for the large domestic mammals from Middle Late Saxon Ipswich

Late Saxon Sites	Cattle %	Sheep/goat %	Pig %	NISP
MLS Ipswich	42.4	27.7	30.7	6579
Flaxengate TIII	60.4	27.0	12.3	1812
Thetford	46.8	33.1	20.1	1963
Coppergate Period 4	57.2	28.3	10.0	9687*
Winchester	43.3	36.1	20.6	3257
Antwerp	37.6	23.7	38.1	2779

*The Coppergate assemblage includes a small percentage of other species.
Data source: O'Connor 2012, table 20.1; O'Connor 1989, table 40; Bourdillon 2009, table 4.1

Table 4.4 Species ratios for cattle, sheep/goat and pig from selected Late Saxon sites

pigs in the Winchester suburbs than there are in Middle Saxon Hamwic (Coy 2009, 54). Once again, the overall species ratios from Middle Late Saxon Ipswich are more similar to those from 8th–10th-century Antwerp than they are to other Late Saxon and Anglo-Scandinavian sites in Britain (see Table 4.4). The low proportion of sheep is particularly striking, given the proximity of Ipswich to the Sandlings region which has historically been associated with the sheep husbandry. In fact, the current ecology of the Sandlings was created by sheep husbandry after the removal of the original tree cover in prehistoric times (The Landscape Partnership 2012). It is possible that some of the pork that was consumed at Middle Late Saxon Ipswich was supplied from non-local sources. Isotopic analyses would be required to answer this question definitively.

III. Domestic Animals from Middle Late Saxon Ipswich

Ipswich experienced rapid growth during the Middle Saxon and Early Late Saxon periods. The 10th century was a period of rapid urbanism in both the Anglo-Saxon regions and the parts of eastern England that remained under Scandinavian control. In East Anglia, Norwich had developed as a centre of regional importance by the 930s (Ayers 2011, 70), and Thetford also developed as a thriving centre for regional trade in the 10th and 11th centuries (Rogerson and Dallas 1984; Dallas 1993). As noted above, however, Ipswich remained one of the ten largest towns during this period. How and to what extent did these changes affect the ways that Ipswich was provisioned with food and other animal products?

	Cattle	% Cattle	Caprine	% Caprine	Pig	% Pig	Horse	% Horse
Skull	22	0.8	22	1.2	98	4.9	0	0.0
Horn Core	142	5.2	197	10.9	0	0.0	0	0.0
Maxilla	6	0.2	10	0.6	12	0.6	0	0.0
Maxillary Teeth	28	1.0	20	1.1	11	0.6	4	13.8
Mandible	86	3.2	131	7.2	157	7.9	1	3.4
Mandibular Teeth	233	8.5	153	8.4	226	11.3	3	10.3
Tooth Fragments	2	0.1	7	0.4	11	0.6	1	3.4
Hyoid	0	0.0	1	0.1	0	0.0	0	0.0
Atlas	1	0.0	7	0.4	3	0.2	1	3.4
Axis	1	0.0	3	0.2	3	0.2	0	0.0
Scapula	75	2.7	112	6.2	109	5.5	3	10.3
Humerus	80	2.9	165	9.1	155	7.8	0	0.0
Radius	173	6.3	166	9.2	114	5.7	0	0.0
Ulna	56	2.1	55	3.0	116	5.8	0	0.0
Carpal	140	5.1	11	0.6	4	0.2	0	0.0
Metacarpus	70	2.6	104	5.7	152	7.6	2	6.9
Innominate	25	0.9	50	2.8	37	1.9	1	3.4
Femur	50	1.8	49	2.7	82	4.1	0	0.0
Patella	5	0.2	1	0.1	0	0.0	0	0.0
Tibia	155	5.7	170	9.4	147	7.4	1	3.4
Fibula	0	0.0	0	0.0	14	0.7	0	0.0
Astragalus	145	5.3	66	3.6	112	5.6	1	3.4
Calcaneus	145	5.3	53	2.9	77	3.9	0	0.0
Other Tarsals	99	3.6	9	0.5	25	1.3	0	0.0
Metatarsus	123	4.5	93	5.1	140	7.0	2	6.9
Metapodium	55	2.0	14	0.8	25	1.3	0	0.0
First Phalanx	349	12.8	112	6.2	133	6.7	3	10.3
Second Phalanx	255	9.3	24	1.3	25	1.3	4	13.8
Third Phalanx	207	7.6	8	0.4	12	0.6	2	6.9

Table 4.5 Body-part distributions based on NISP for the large domestic mammals from Middle Late Saxon Ipswich

Domestic Mammals

The body-part distributions for the main domestic mammals from the Middle Late Saxon contexts in Ipswich are shown in Table 4.5. The phalanges, carpals and tarsals of the smaller species are clearly underrepresented due to the absence of fine screening. The Middle Late Saxon body-part distributions show no real changes from the Middle Saxon and Early Late Saxon periods.

Cattle remain the most numerous species throughout the 10th century, and they would have provided the bulk of the meat that was consumed at Ipswich. The age profiles based on epiphyseal fusion of the long bones are shown in Table 4.6, and the age profile based on dental eruption and wear is shown in Figure 4.2. The epiphyseal fusion data indicate that just over half the cattle survived to more than 3.5 to 4 years of age. In comparison the Early Late Saxon cattle were culled as slightly younger animals; only 40% of those cattle survived to more than 3.5–4 years. The dental ageing data, on the other hand, provide evidence for more young, market-age cattle. The number of complete ageable mandibles from the Middle Late Saxon features is small, but there are few cattle with heavily worn molars. There are also very few examples of possible traction pathologies; only three cattle bones showed evidence for exostoses. These data suggest that the inhabitants of Ipswich were provisioned with a mix of market-age and older cattle, but with very few elderly animals that had spent their lives pulling ploughs. By way of contrast, the Late Saxon fauna from the Winchester suburbs produced a large number of young calves (Coy 2009, 48), something that is not seen in either the Middle Saxon or Late Saxon assemblages from Ipswich.

The measurement data for the Middle Late Saxon cattle from Ipswich are shown in Table 4.7. All the measurements are, on average, slightly smaller than the cattle measurements recorded for the Middle Saxon and Early Late Saxon cattle. Two factors may be in play here. First, fewer oxen may have been sent to market in the Middle Late Saxon period. While the numbers are small, it

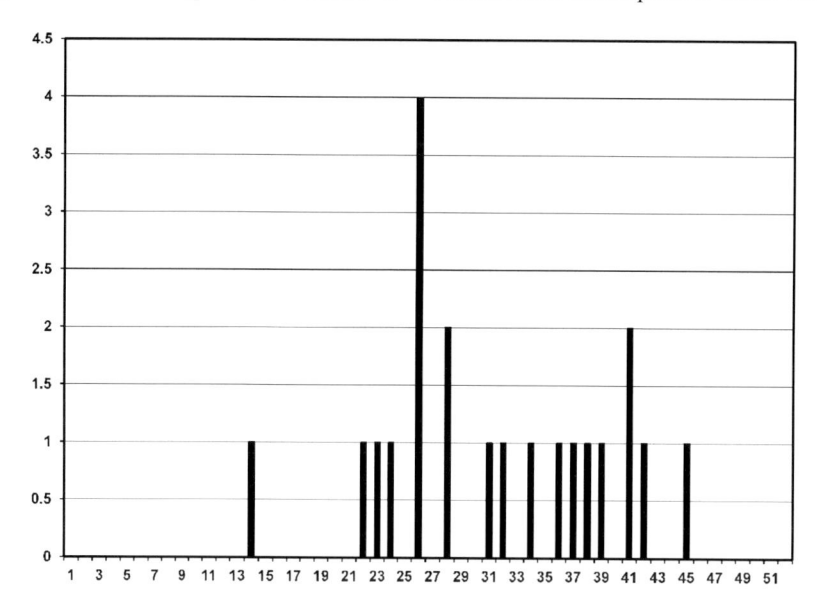

Figure 4.2 Mandible Wear Stages for cattle mandibles from Middle Late Saxon Ipswich

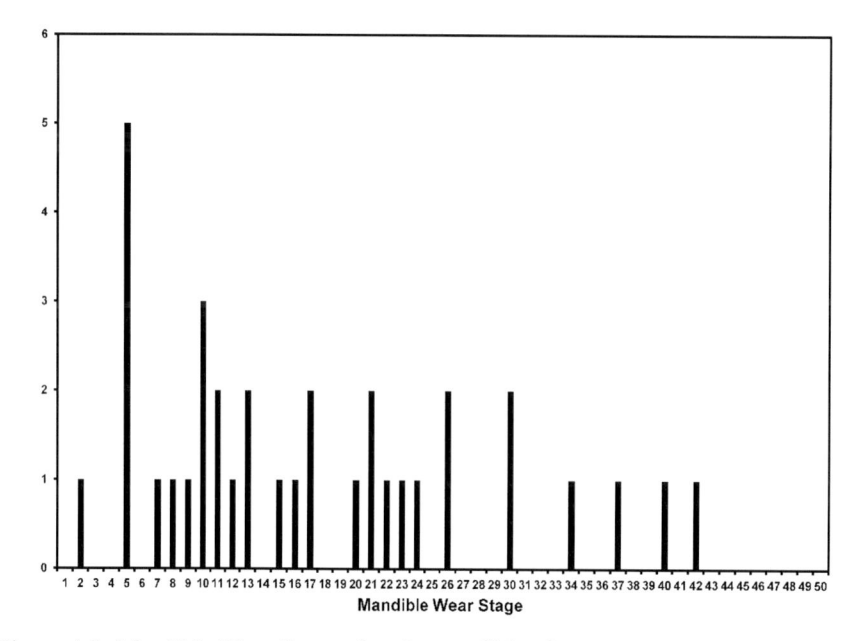

Figure 4.3 Mandible Wear Stages for pig mandibles from Middle Late Saxon Ipswich

Measurement	Mean	Min.	Max.	S	C.V.	N
Radius Bp	76.8	65.1	86.0	4.8	6.5	36
Metacarpus GL	188.9	172.0	207.0	9.1	4.8	47
Metacarpus Bd	56.2	50.0	71.0	5.0	8.9	68
Tibia Bd	57.4	49.2	67.9	4.6	8.1	90
Astragalus GLl	61.5	53.3	72.4	3.9	6.3	108
Metatarsus GL	212.7	191.0	244.5	13.1	6.2	31
Metatarsus Bd	51.6	44.0	60.6	4.6	8.9	77
Withers Height (cm)	114.8	104.1	133.3	5.8	5.1	81

Table 4.7 Measurement data for Middle Late Saxon cattle from Ipswich

	N. Fused	N. Unfused	% Unfused
7–18 months			
D. Scapula	52	0	0
D. Humerus	61	6	9
P. Radius	75	2	3
Total	188	8	4
24–36 months			
D. Metacarpus	39	21	35
D. Tibia	79	63	44
D. Metatarsus	76	39	34
Total	194	123	39
36–42 months			
P. Calcaneus	45	72	62
42–48 months			
P. Humerus	0	1	100
D. Radius	48	48	50
P. Ulna	9	19	68
P. Femur	3	2	40
D. Femur	18	19	50
Total	78	89	53

Table 4.6 Epiphyseal fusion data for cattle from Middle Late Saxon Ipswich; ages are based on Silver (1969)

	N. Fused	N. Unfused	% Unfused
12 months			
D. Scapula	42	20	32
D. Humerus	100	40	29
P. Radius	67	8	11
Total	209	68	25
24 months			
D. Metacarpus	24	124	84
D. Tibia	46	75	62
Total	70	199	74
24–30 months			
D. Metatarsus	29	98	77
P. Calcaneus	15	82	85
D. Fibula	1	4	80
Total	45	184	80
36–42 months			
P. Humerus	0	16	100
D. Radius	8	53	87
P. Ulna	4	84	95
P. Femur	0	5	100
D. Femur	6	59	91
P. Tibia	2	17	89
P. Fibula	0	2	100
Total	20	236	92

Table 4.8 Epiphyseal fusion data for pigs from Middle Late Saxon Ipswich; ages are based on Silver (1969)

is worth noting that all the Middle Late Saxon cattle included in the Principal Components Analysis were female. Second, we may be seeing a long term trend towards a decrease in cattle size. We will return to this question in the final chapter of this volume.

Pigs are the second most common animal species at Middle Late Saxon Ipswich, and they would have been second to cattle in terms of their meat yield. Age profiles for the Middle Late Saxon pigs based on epiphyseal fusion are shown in Table 4.8, and the kill-pattern based on dental eruption and wear is shown in Figure 4.3. The data based on dental eruption and wear indicate that the 10th-century inhabitants of Ipswich consumed a small number of very young pigs whose first molars were not fully erupted. These pigs were young animals that were under 6 months of age when they were sent to market. The assemblage also includes a large number of market-age animals and a small number of very elderly animals that were probably sent to market when they were no longer needed for breeding. The epiphyseal data yield similar results. Only one-quarter of pigs were culled during their first year of life; an additional 50% of the pigs were killed by 24 months, and a full 80% of the pigs were sent to market by the age of 2.5 years. Only a small portion of the animals survived to more than 4 years.

The measurements taken on pig bones from Middle Late Saxon sites are shown in Table 4.9. All the lower third molars fall well within the domestic pig range. A single complete radius yielded a withers height estimate of 71.7cm. These pigs are similar in size to the Middle Saxon pigs from Hamwic which had estimated withers heights of 63.2 to 77.8cm (Bourdillon and Coy 1980, 112). They are also similar in size to the Middle Saxon pigs from Brandon (71.1–74.7cm) and Wicken Bonhunt (65.1–77.9cm) (Crabtree 2012, 52).

Measurement	Mean	Min.	Max	S	C.V.	N
Radius Bp	27.1	23.2	30.9	1.9	6.8	34
Tibia Bd	28.3	25.7	31.9	1.6	5.7	27
Astragalus GLl	38.3	33.7	43.0	2.1	5.5	49
Lower M3 Length	31.1	26.6	33.7	1.8	5.6	14
Withers Heights	*GL (mm)*	*WH (cm)*				
Radius	136.4	71.7				

Table 4.9 Measurements taken on pig bones from Middle Late Saxon Ipswich

Sheep are third in importance for Middle Late Saxon Ipswich based on NISP, following cattle and pigs. Sheep are slightly more numerous than they were in Middle Saxon Ipswich, and they are more numerous than they were in Early Late Saxon Ipswich if we exclude the St Nicholas Street site (4201). It is possible that the increasing numbers of sheep may be linked to more widespread wool production in East Anglia at this time.

The measurements taken on the caprine remains from Middle Late Saxon Ipswich are shown in Table 4.10. These sheep have an average estimated withers height of 60.5cm, almost identical to the average estimated withers height of the Early Late Saxon sheep (60.3cm). These sheep are similar in size to the late Roman sheep from Icklingham and the Early Saxon sheep from West Stow (Crabtree 2012, 52, table 5.4). They are larger than the Middle Saxon sheep from Ipswich and Brandon. The data from Late Saxon Winchester and Middle Saxon Hamwic show just the opposite pattern. The Hamwic Middle Saxon sheep had an average estimated withers height of 61.7cm, while the Late Saxon sheep from the Winchester northern and western suburbs had an average estimated withers height of only 55cm (range 51–62cm) (Bourdillon 2009, 70). These small sheep are comparable in size to the

Measurement	Mean	Min.	Max.	S	C.V.	N
Radius GL	153.4	141.6	168.5	7.4	4.8	22
Radius Bp	31.8	27.1	36.4	2.0	6.3	57
Metacarpus GL	122.9	112.5	137.4	6.1	5.4	37
Metacarpus Bd	25.7	22.0	30.5	1.4	5.4	57
Tibia Bd	26.3	21.7	29.9	1.3	4.9	107
Astragalus GLl	28.5	24.7	32.8	1.5	5.2	37
Metatarsus GL	133.0	117.5	142.4	6.4	5.7	32
Metatarsus Bd	24.3	21.6	27.8	1.1	4.4	57
Withers Height (cm)	60.5	53.3	67.7	3.0	5.0	93

Table 4.10 Measurements taken on sheep/goat remains from Middle Late Saxon Ipswich

	N. Fused	N. Unfused	% Fused	Age of Fusion
Scapula distal	77	12	13	6–8 mo.
Humerus distal	134	10	7	10 mo.
Radius proximal	104	9	8	10 mo.
Total early fusing	**315**	**31**	**9**	
Tibia distal	124	19	13	1.5–2 yrs
Metacarpus distal	62	26	30	1.5–2 yrs
Metatarsus distal	66	14	18	20–28 mo.
Total middle fusing	**252**	**59**	**19**	
Ulna proximal	18	21	54	2.5 yrs
Femur proximal	1	4	80	2.5–3 yrs
Calcaneus tuber	33	12	27	2.5–3 yrs
Radius distal	57	28	33	3 yrs
Humerus proximal	3	6	67	3–3.5 yrs
Femur distal	19	26	58	3–3.5 yrs
Total late fusing	**131**	**97**	**43**	

Table 4.11 Epiphyseal fusion data for Middle Late Saxon sheep from Ipswich; ages are based on Silver (1969)

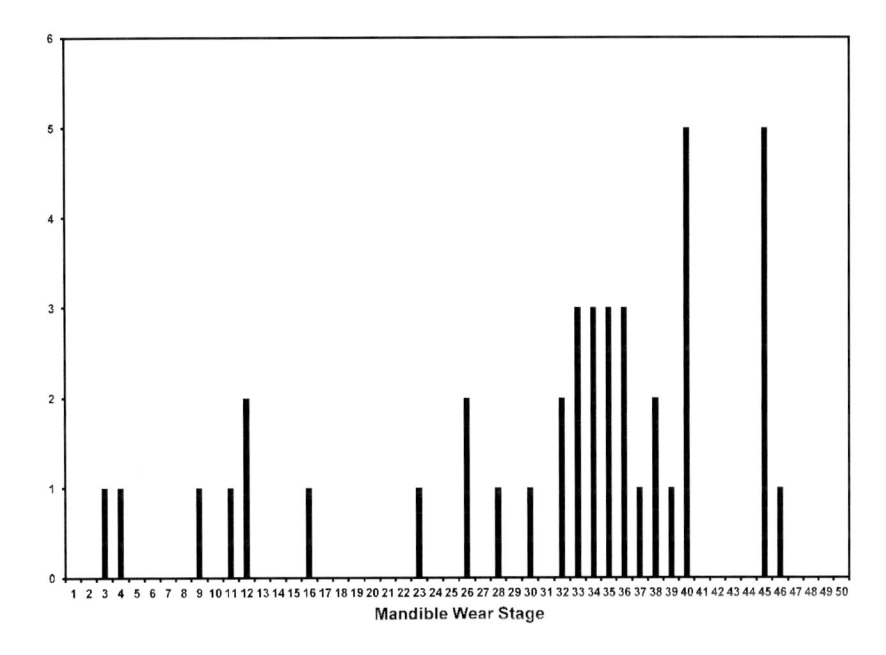

Figure 4.4 Mandible Wear Stages for sheep and goat mandibles from Middle Late Saxon Ipswich

Middle Saxon sheep from Brandon and Ipswich. Bourdillon (2009, 70) compares these small sheep to the post-conquest wool sheep of Wessex, but she notes that the Winchester sheep show a wider range of ages than would be expected from a wool flock.

The age profile based on dental eruption and wear for the Middle Late Saxon sheep is shown in Figure 4.4, and the epiphyseal fusion data are shown in Table 4.11. While a small number of young sheep are included in the assemblages, most of the animals were market-aged sheep and older animals that were sent to market after they were no longer needed for wool, milk and breeding.

Only one complete horse long bone was recovered from the Middle Late Saxon deposits in Ipswich. A single metacarpus with a greatest length (GL) of 247.9mm yielded a withers height estimate of 129.6cm. This horse is similar in size to the horses that were recovered from the Middle Saxon and Early Late Saxon deposits. Coy (2009, 50) notes that most of the horses from the western suburbs of Late Saxon Winchester were the size of large, sturdy ponies.

A few measurable dog bones were also recovered from the Middle Late Saxon contexts (Table 4.12). Two femora that appear to belong to the same individual yielded withers height estimates of about 40cm. A third femur was from a larger dog that is similar in size to the smallest of the Early Saxon and Middle Saxon dogs from East Anglia. Even though only a small number of measurable dog bones was recovered from the Ipswich Middle Late Saxon

Element	GL (mm)	WH (cm)
Femur	134.5	40.5
Femur	134.0	40.3
Fenur	170.4	51.3

Withers heights (in cm) were calculated using Koudelka's factors following von den Driesch and Boessneck (1974)

Table 4.12 Measurements (in mm) taken on complete dog long bones from Middle Late Saxon Ipswich

assemblage, these bones show some of the size diversity seen in the larger Early Late Saxon dog assemblage.

Domestic Birds

Chickens are far more common than domestic geese in the Middle Late Saxon deposits from Ipswich; chickens make up 93% of the domestic birds from the Middle Late Saxon deposits at Ipswich. Chicken bones also make up a large majority of the domestic bird remains from the Late Saxon suburbs of Winchester (Bourdillon 2009, 79). While chicken bones were recovered from nearly all the Middle Late Saxon sites in Ipswich, most of the chicken bones were recovered from the St Peter's Street site (5203). The Middle Late Saxon chicken bone measurements are summarised in Table 4.13.

Measurement	Mean	Min.	Max.	S	C.V.	N
Humerus GL	66.5	55.4	84.2	5.6	8.4	75
Radius GL	64.0	56.7	68.7	5.8	9.1	13
Ulna GL	67.4	58.7	81.9	6.0	8.9	32
Femur GL	75.4	63.6	83.6	5.4	7.2	53
Tibiotarsus GL	102.9	90.6	116.3	7.5	7.3	84
Tarsometatarsus GL	69.4	56.5	81.2	6.1	8.8	33

Table 4.13 Measurements taken on chicken bones from Middle Late Saxon Ipswich

IV. Provisioning Middle Late Saxon Ipswich

Despite the political turmoil of the 10th century, there are very few changes in urban provisioning between the Early Late Saxon and the Middle Late Saxon periods in Ipswich. The species ratios, age profiles and biometrical data point to long-term continuities in urban diet and animal use throughout the late 9th and 10th centuries.

Chapter 5. Animal Bones from Early Medieval Ipswich

I. Introduction

The faunal remains from the Early Medieval deposits in Ipswich date from the 11th and the first half of the 12th centuries. These deposits span the end of Anglo-Saxon England and the start of Norman rule. While the Norman Conquest did not lead to fundamental changes in ceramic types and house forms in Ipswich, it did have devastating effects on the city as a whole. As noted in Chapter 1, by the end of the 12th century, many of the urban plots in Ipswich lay in waste, and Ipswich was no longer among the ten largest towns in England. Sykes (2007) has shown that the Norman Conquest led to some changes in animal exploitation in eastern England. Two of the animals that were introduced around AD 1000 were the rabbit and the fallow deer, and there is evidence for fallow deer from the Early Medieval deposits in Ipswich. The question I hope to answer is whether we can see other changes in animal husbandry patterns and hunting practices in Early Medieval Ipswich.

II. The Composition of the Early Medieval Faunal Assemblage from Ipswich

Twelve sites produced faunal remains that could be dated to the Early Medieval period in Ipswich. Most of the animal bones were recovered from pits, but the faunal remains from the Bridge Street site (6202) were recovered from a series of layers that could be dated to the Early Medieval period, and some of the material from the Buttermarket/St Stephen's Lane site (3104) came from a cellared building. The animal bones recovered from the Early Medieval deposits are shown in Table 5.1. The amphibian remains that were recovered from the Early Medieval deposits have been included in the Appendix Table 10. The Early Medieval animal bones are primarily those of domestic mammals and birds. Hunting and fowling continued to play only minor roles in the Early Medieval economy. Hunted mammals include small numbers of red deer, roe deer, fallow deer and hares, as well as single bones of a fox and a whale.

Site No.	5801	1804	0802	3410	6202	5901	5902	4201	4801	4601	5203	3104	Total
Species													
Domestic Mammals													
Cattle (*Bos taurus*)	422	39	248	226	573	62	38	90	413	200	671	960	2942
Sheep (*Ovis aries*)	6	0	10	0	20	4	2	4	9	39	17	18	129
Goat (*Capra hircus*)	2	0	1	2	3	2	0	2	5	11	2	14	44
Sheep/Goat	102	35	88	134	547	31	29	56	240	220	435	489	2406
Pig (*Sus scrofa*)	310	29	190	299	376	45	33	135	182	127	404	544	2674
Horse (*Equus caballus*)	0	0	0	2	12	0	0	3	9	9	7	10	52
Dog (*Canis familiaris*)	0	0	0	2	19	45	0	13	8	11	25	9	132
Cat (*Felis catus*)	0	2	0	0	3	0	0	1	2	10	2	4	24
Wild Mammals													
Red Deer (*Cervus elaphus*)	1	0	0	0	4	0	0	5	0	1	2	2	15
Roe Deer (*Capreolus capreolus*)	0	0	0	0	1	0	0	0	0	5	0	1	7
Fallow Deer (*Dama dama*)	0	0	0	0	0	0	0	2	0	0	0	0	2
Hare (*Lepus* sp.)	0	0	0	1	0	0	0	0	1	15	0	6	23
Fox (*Vulpes vulpes*)	0	0	0	0	0	0	0	0	0	1	0	0	1
Whale (Cetacea)	0	0	0	0	1	0	0	0	0	0	0	0	1
Domestic Birds													
Chicken (*Gallus gallus*)	40	3	27	36	76	15	7	56	94	15	55	223	647
Goose (*Anser anser*)	1	1	7	11	6	0	0	12	17	0	10	24	89
Wild Birds													
Mallard (*Anas platyrhynchos*)	0	0	0	2	2	0	0	0	2	0	0	2	8
Teal (*Anus anus*)	0	0	0	2	0	0	0	0	0	0	0	0	2
Pigeons (*Columba* sp.)	0	0	0	0	0	0	0	0	0	2	0	0	2
Raven (*Corvus corax*)	0	0	0	0	0	0	0	0	0	0	0	1	0
Sparrow Hawk (*Accipiter nisus*)	0	0	0	0	0	0	0	1	0	0	0	0	1
Cormorants (*Phalacrocorax* sp.)	0	0	0	0	1	0	0	0	0	0	0	0	1
Total	884	109	571	717	1644	204	109	379	983	666	1630	2307	10203

Table 5.1 List of bird and mammal remains recovered from Early Medieval sites in Ipswich

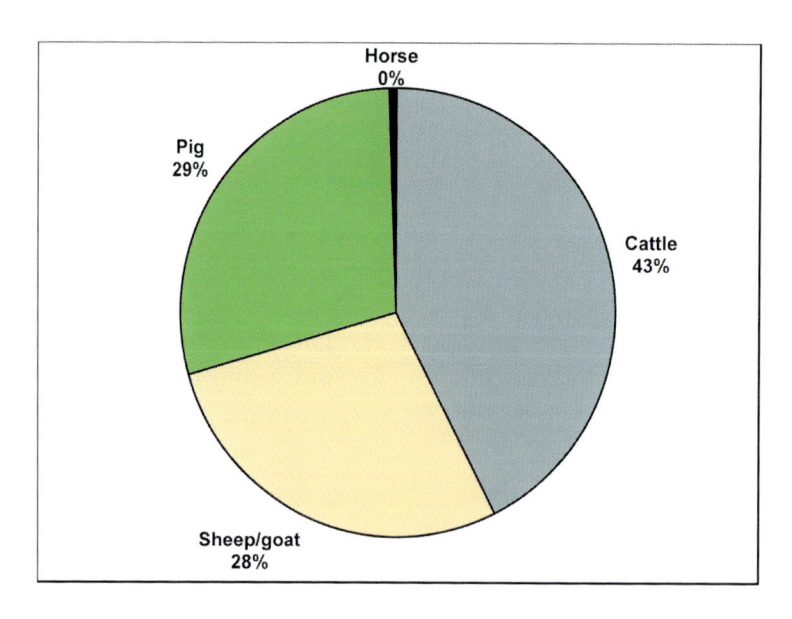

Figure 5.1 Species ratios based on NISP for the large domestic mammal remains from Early Medieval Ipswich

	NISP	%NISP
Cattle	3942	42.6
Sheep/goat	2579	27.9
Pig	2674	28.9
Horse	52	0.6

Table 5.2 Species ratios for the large domestic mammals from Early Medieval Ipswich

The bird remains are mostly bones of domestic chickens which outnumber domestic geese by a ratio of more than 7 to 1; chickens make up nearly 88% of the domestic bird remains. While this proportion is slightly less than the proportion of chickens in the Middle Late Saxon assemblage, it is twice as high as the proportion of chickens in the Middle Saxon assemblage. The most common wild species are mallard ducks, followed by small numbers of pigeon and teal bones. Single bones of a

	Cattle	% Cattle	Caprine	% Caprine	Pig	% Pig	Horse	% Horse
Skull	68	1.8	74	2.7	285	10.8	2	3.8
Horn Core	155	4.1	174	6.3	0	0.0	0	0.0
Maxilla	46	1.2	21	0.8	59	2.2	0	0.0
Maxillary Teeth	117	3.1	47	1.7	60	2.3	1	1.9
Mandible	262	6.9	343	12.4	258	9.8	1	1.9
Mandibular Teeth	331	8.7	220	8.0	252	9.6	12	23.1
Tooth Fragments	33	0.9	14	0.5	43	1.6	1	1.9
Hyoid	2	0.1	2	0.1	0	0.0	0	0.0
Atlas	12	0.3	7	0.3	7	0.3	0	0.0
Axis	5	0.1	4	0.1	3	0.1	1	1.9
Scapula	114	3.0	151	5.5	190	7.2	2	3.8
Humerus	146	3.8	189	6.8	156	5.9	2	3.8
Radius	198	5.2	166	6.0	130	4.9	3	5.8
Ulna	82	2.2	60	2.2	139	5.3	1	1.9
Carpal	128	3.4	3	0.1	3	0.1	1	1.9
Metacarpus	169	4.4	187	6.8	175	6.6	2	3.8
Innominate	93	2.4	102	3.7	69	2.6	1	1.9
Femur	74	1.9	59	2.1	71	2.7	1	1.9
Patella	9	0.2	0	0.0	0	0.0	0	0.0
Tibia	197	5.2	272	9.9	153	5.8	2	3.8
Fibula	0	0.0	0	0.0	44	1.7	0	0.0
Astragalus	172	4.5	62	2.2	114	4.3	0	0.0
Calcaneus	165	4.3	60	2.2	77	2.9	2	3.8
Other Tarsals	91	2.4	8	0.3	14	0.5	2	3.8
Metatarsus	178	4.7	168	6.1	143	5.4	2	3.8
Metapodium	103	2.7	42	1.5	45	1.7	3	5.8
First Phalanx	409	10.8	187	6.8	98	3.7	3	5.8
Second Phalanx	249	6.6	126	4.6	37	1.4	2	3.8
Third Phalanx	193	5.1	13	0.5	9	0.3	5	9.6

Table 5.3 Body-part distributions based on NISP for the large domestic mammals from Early Medieval Ipswich

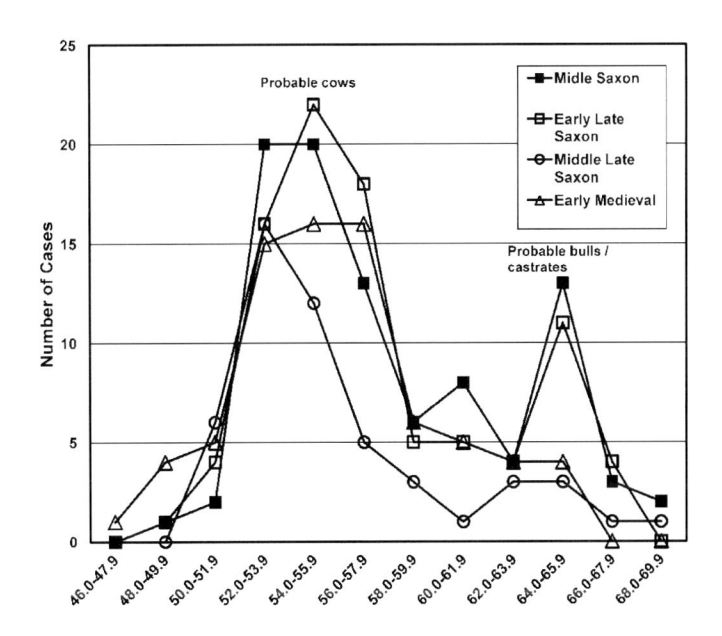

Figure 5.2 Distribution of distal tibial breadths (Bd) for Middle Saxon, Early Late Saxon, Middle Late Saxon and Early Medieval cattle from Ipswich. Note the higher numbers of possible males in Middle Saxon and Early Late Saxon assemblages

raven, a sparrow hawk, and a cormorant were also identified. As noted above, ravens and other corvids can thrive and prosper in urban environments. The striking feature of all the faunal assemblages from Saxon and Early Medieval Ipswich is the absence of the numerous water birds and waders that are found in most rural assemblages from Anglo-Saxon East Anglia.

III. Domestic Animals from Early Medieval Ipswich

The species ratios for the main domestic mammals are shown in Figure 5.1 and Table 5.2. The rank order of the species remains unchanged. Cattle are the most common species, followed by pigs and caprines, with only a very small number of horse remains. The one change that is visible is a gradual increase in the proportion of sheep/goats in the assemblage through time. The caprine proportion rises from approximately 23% in the Middle Saxon period to 28% in the Early Medieval assemblages.

The body-part distributions for the large domestic mammals are shown in Table 5.3. The small elements, such as carpals, tarsals, and phalanges from sheep/goats and pigs, are clearly underrepresented as a result of hand collection of the fauna.

Domestic Mammals

The measurement data for the Early Medieval cattle are shown in Table 5.4. The biometric data suggest that there is a gradual decrease in the lengths of the long bones through time. As noted above, fewer male cattle were sent to market during the Middle Late Saxon and Early Medieval periods. This can be seen in the Principal Components Analysis (Chapter 2), and it is also apparent in the distribution of the distal tibial breadths (Bd) as seen in Figure 5.2. Changing sex ratios, however, do not completely explain the decreases in cattle bone lengths through time. The smallest female Early Medieval cattle are clearly smaller than their Middle Saxon and Early Late Saxon counterparts. This can be seen in the distributions of cattle withers heights shown in Figure 5.3.

The ageing data for cattle based on dental eruption and wear are shown in Figure 5.4, and the data based on epiphyseal fusion of the long bones are shown in Table 5.5. The number of ageable mandibles is relatively small, but they include both market-aged and older adult cattle. The epiphyseal fusion data present a similar picture. Almost no cattle were sent to market in the first 18 months of life. About one-third of the cattle were culled between two and three years of age, and half survived to more than four years.

Measurement	Mean	Min.	Max.	S	C.V.	N
Radius Bp	74.2	64.0	85.8	6.4	8.6	27
Metacarpus GL	182.0	158.5	201.9	9.3	5.1	27
Metacarpus Bd	55.6	47.4	67.8	5.9	10.7	45
Tibia Bd	56.0	46.9	65.2	4.0	7.1	76
Astragalus GLl	60.1	50.4	68.2	3.4	5.7	96
Metatarsus GL	208.3	196.5	224.5	6.9	3.3	20
Metatarsus Bd	51.0	43.5	64.6	5.1	10.0	58
Withers Height (cm)	112.3	97.1	123.7	5.0	4.5	49

Table 5.4 Measurements taken on Early Medieval cattle from Ipswich

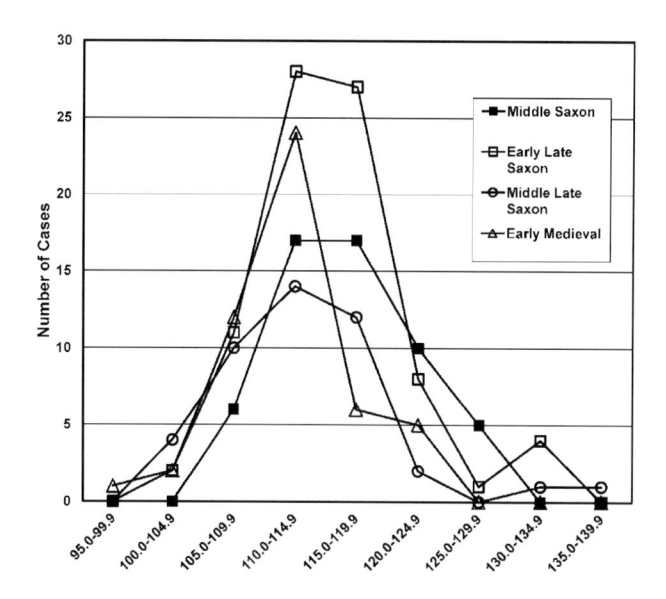

Figure 5.3 Distribution of withers heights for Middle Saxon, Early Late Saxon, Middle Late Saxon and Early Medieval cattle from Ipswich

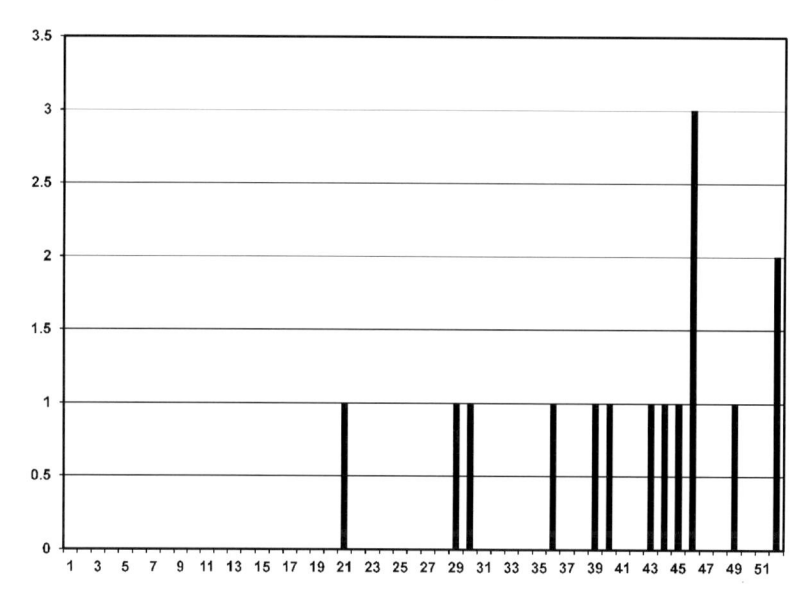

Figure 5.4 Distribution of Mandible Wear Stages for Early Medieval cattle mandibles from Ipswich

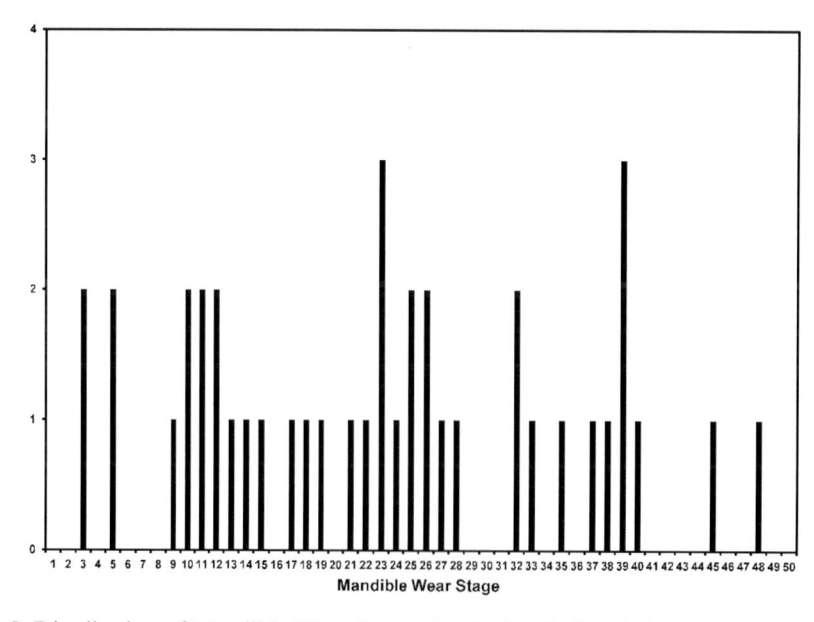

Figure 5.5 Distribution of Mandible Wear Stages for Early Medieval pig mandibles from Ipswich

	N. Fused	N. Unfused	% Unfused
7–18 months			
D. Scapula	51	0	0
D. Humerus	78	9	10
P. Radius	81	0	0
Total	210	9	4
24–36 months			
D. Metacarpus	63	37	35
D. Tibia	98	37	27
D. Metatarsus	71	35	33
Total	232	109	32
36–42 months			
P. Calcaneus	40	64	62
42–48 months			
P. Humerus	3	2	40
D. Radius	43	45	51
P. Ulna	6	10	63
P. Femur	7	13	65
D. Femur	17	16	48
Total	76	86	53

Table 5.5 Ageing data for Early Medieval cattle based on epiphyseal fusion of the long bones; ages are based on Silver (1969)

	N. Fused	N. Unfused	% Unfused
12 months			
D. Scapula	74	16	18
D. Humerus	82	17	17
P. Radius	69	3	4
Total	225	36	14
24 months			
D. Metacarpus	30	80	73
D. Tibia	48	58	55
Total	78	138	64
24–30 months			
D. Metatarsus	15	71	83
P. Calcaneus	11	62	85
D. Fibula	0	3	100
Total	26	136	84
36–42 months			
P. Humerus	1	9	90
D. Radius	1	32	97
P. Ulna	4	62	94
P. Femur	0	5	100
D. Femur	2	36	95
P. Tibia	3	20	87
P. Fibula	0	1	100
Total	11	165	94

Table 5.7 Epiphyseal fusion data for pigs from Early Medieval Ipswich; ages are based on Silver (1969)

While pigs are second in importance to cattle in the Early Medieval assemblages, the numbers of pig bones are only slightly higher than the numbers of caprine bones. The measurements taken on the Early Medieval pig bones are shown in Table 5.6, and a single complete radius provided a withers height estimate 65.5cm. The third molar lengths indicate that all the Early Medieval pigs were domestic swine, and the other measurements are essentially unchanged from the Middle and Late Saxon periods.

The age profile for pigs based on dental eruption and wear is shown in Figure 5.5, and the ageing data based on epiphyseal fusion of the long bones is shown in Table 5.7. Both sets of data show that a small number of pigs were sent to market in the first year of life. Nearly two thirds of the pigs were culled by two years of age, and all but about 16% were culled by 2.5 years. Very few pigs survived to advanced years. This is exactly the cull pattern that we would expect from a market economy. Most of the pigs were culled in later adolescence after they had gained substantial amounts of weight. There is little profit in continuing to feed a pig beyond this point. The few elderly pigs that were sent to market were probably breeding stock whose productivity had fallen off.

The age profiles for sheep based on dental eruption and wear are shown in Figure 5.6, and the profiles based on epiphyseal fusion are shown in Table 5.8. When the dental age profiles are grouped into broader classes (see Crabtree 1990, table 46), some changes in the sheep/goat mortality patterns through time become apparent (Fig. 5.7). While the Middle Saxon age profile includes a large number of sheep that were sent to market at ages 6–12 months, the Middle Late Saxon and Early Medieval assemblages include more market-aged and older sheep. The Early Medieval assemblage includes a large number of market-aged animals that were sent to market at 2–4 years of age, while the Middle Late Saxon assemblage includes a larger proportion of older sheep in the 4–8 year old class. None of the assemblages includes the elderly 8–10 year old sheep that are present in Anglo-Saxon rural

Measurement	Mean	Min.	Max	S	C.V.	N
Radius Bp	27.8	25.5	31.2	1.3	4.7	29
Tibia Bd	29.0	24.0	33.4	1.8	6.2	38
Astragalus GL1	38.2	34.2	42.0	1.9	4.9	44
Lower M3 Length	31.4	28.4	37.8	2.4	7.5	22
Withers Heights	*GL (mm)*	*WH (cm)*				
Tibia	167.0	65.5				

Table 5.6 Measurements taken on pig bones from Early Medieval Ipswich

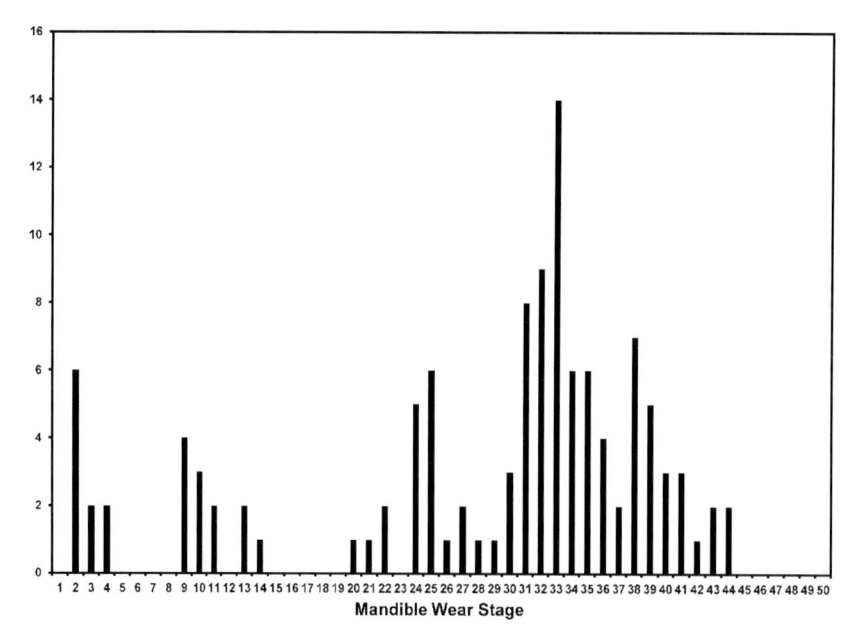

Figure 5.6 Distribution of Mandible Wear Stages for Early Medieval sheep and goat mandibles from Ipswich

	N. Fused	N. Unfused	% Fused	Age of Fusion
Scapula distal	77	8	9	6–8 mo.
Humerus distal	118	8	6	10 mo.
Radius proximal	82	2	2	10 mo.
Total early fusing	**277**	**18**	**6**	
Tibia distal	160	25	14	1.5–2 yrs
Metacarpus distal	50	17	25	1.5–2 yrs
Metatarsus distal	69	20	22	20–28 mo.
Total middle fusing	**279**	**62**	**18**	
Ulna proximal	12	8	40	2.5 yrs
Femur proximal	3	11	85	2.5–3 yrs
Calcaneus tuber	31	13	30	2.5–3 yrs
Radius distal	22	24	53	3 yrs
Humerus proximal	3	4	57	3–3.5 yrs
Femur distal	17	23	58	3–3.5 yrs
Total late fusing	**88**	**83**	**48**	

Table 5.8 Epiphyseal fusion data for Early Medieval sheep from Ipswich; ages are based on Silver (1969)

Measurement	Mean	Min.	Max.	S	C.V.	N
Radius GL	152.2	145.6	155.4	3.2	2.1	7
Radius Bp	30.9	27.0	34.5	1.8	5.8	34
Metacarpus GL	123.4	114.3	134.8	4.3	4.3	30
Metacarpus Bd	25.2	22.8	28.0	1.2	4.8	39
Tibia Bd	26.4	22.8	29.6	1.4	5.3	140
Astragalus GLl	28.9	26.0	32.4	1.6	5.5	31
Metatarsus GL	129.0	109.6	148.4	9.0	7.0	40
Metatarsus Bd	23.7	21.0	26.9	1.2	5.1	65
Withers Height (cm)	59.5	49.7	67.4	3.6	6.1	82

Table 5.9 Measurements taken on sheep/goat remains from Early Medieval Ipswich

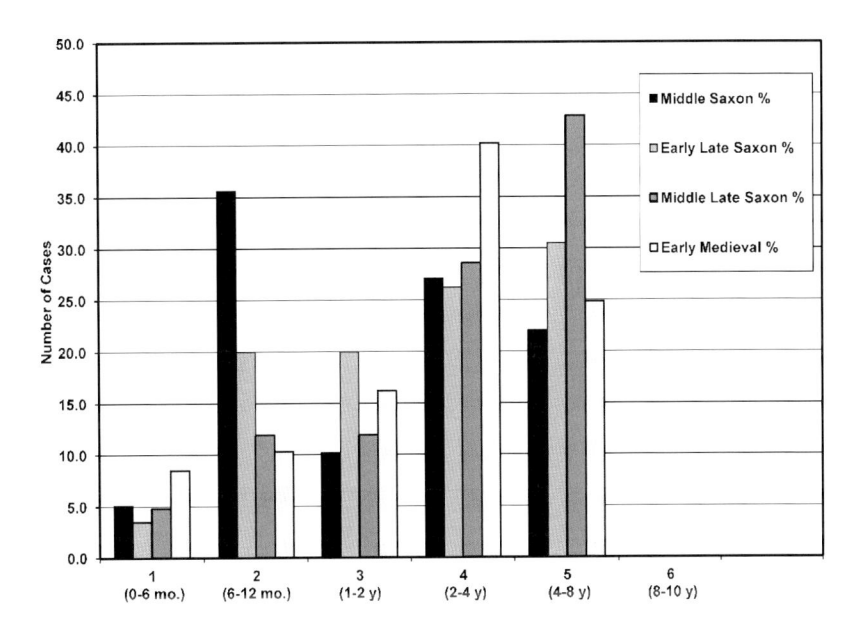

Figure 5.7 Age classes based on dental eruption and wear for sheep and goats from Middle Saxon, Early Late Saxon, Middle Late Saxon and Early Medieval Ipswich

Element	GL (mm)	WH (cm)
Radius	160.1	51.6
Radius	117.9	38.0
Femur	120.8	36.4
Fenur	143.1	43.1

Withers heights (in cm) were calculated using Koudelka's factors following von den Driesch and Boessneck (1974)

Table 5.10 Measurements taken on dog bones from Early Medieval Ipswich

sites such as Brandon and West Stow (Crabtree and Campana 2014, 302, fig. 10.6).

The measurement data for the Early Medieval sheep from Ipswich are shown in Table 5.9. The mean estimated withers height for the Early Medieval sheep is 59.5cm. The Anglo-Scandinavian sheep from 10th–11th-century contexts in York also had a mean estimated withers height of 59cm (O'Connor 1989, 176).

Only 52 horse bones were recovered from the Early Medieval contexts in Ipswich. The assemblage included only one complete long bone. A single metacarpus with a greatest length (GL) of 224.9cm yielded a withers height estimate of 138.7cm. Although the numbers of measurable horse bones in the Ipswich assemblages are limited, there is no evidence for size change between the Middle Saxon and the Early Medieval periods.

The Early Medieval dog remains from Ipswich continue to show the diversity that was apparent in the Late Saxon dogs. Withers height estimates for the Early Medieval dogs range from approximately 36 to 52cm (Table 5.10.

Domestic Birds
The striking features of the bird assemblages from Ipswich are both the large numbers of chickens relative to all other domestic and wild birds and the increase in the proportion of domestic chickens relative to domestic geese between the Middle Saxon period and the Late Saxon and Early Medieval periods. As noted above, by the Early Medieval period, chickens outnumber geese by a ratio of more than 7 to 1. The measurements taken on the chicken bones from Early Medieval Ipswich are shown in Table 5.11

Z-scores were calculated for the greatest lengths (GL) of the humerus, ulna, femur and tibiotarsus (Fig. 5.8). The distributions of the z-scores show a clear bimodality. The humerus, radius and tibiotarsus measurements include a large number of smaller chickens and a smaller number of larger ones, but the ulnae include a larger number of large birds. The explanation for this is not clear. If this bimodality reflects sexual dimorphism, we would expect a large number of smaller female chickens and a much smaller number of cocks and capons, especially if the chickens were kept primarily for their eggs rather than for meat.

Measurement	Mean	Min.	Max.	S	C.V.	N
Humerus GL	67.0	59.3	75.7	4.7	7.1	38
Radius GL	64.4	58.1	71.8	4.3	6.6	8
Ulna GL	67.9	59.0	76.4	5.0	7.4	45
Femur GL	73.6	64.6	82.8	4.6	6.3	33
Tibiotarsus GL	100.9	88.5	112.6	10.3	10.2	96
Tarsometatarsus GL	67.6	59.6	78.2	4.6	6.8	25

Table 5.11 Measurements taken on chicken bones from Early Medieval Ipswich

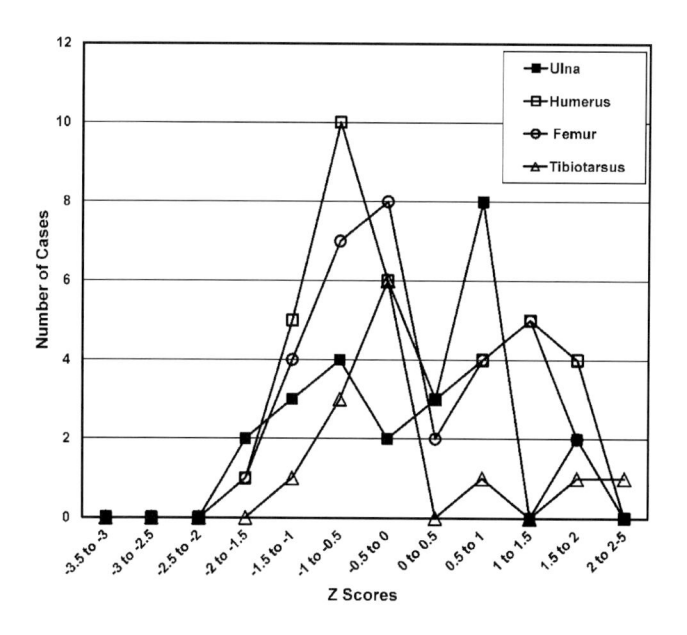

Figure 5.8 Z-scores calculated for the greatest lengths (GL) of chicken humeri, ulnae, femora and tibiotarsi from Early Medieval Ipswich

IV. Provisioning Early Medieval Ipswich

Ipswich clearly suffered in the aftermath of the Norman Conquest, but the archaeozoological data do not indicate marked changes in urban provisioning. The overall changes that are apparent are relatively minor. There is evidence for a slight increase in sheep and goats, and more of these animals appeared to have been culled at 2–4 years of age. Although the percentage of chickens in the Early Medieval period is slightly less than the proportion seen in the Late Saxon periods, chickens are far more common than they are in the Middle Saxon period. Chickens could have provided both eggs and meat for the Early Medieval inhabitants of Ipswich. We will return to the question of why chickens may have played such an important role in the provisioning of Late Saxon and Early Medieval Ipswich in Chapter 6.

Chapter 6. Conclusions and Future Directions

I. Introduction

The goal of this chapter is to explore long-term changes and continuities in urban provisioning in Ipswich from the Middle Saxon through the Early Medieval period. In particular, did the residents of Ipswich obtain their meat through markets, or were they provisioned by other more indirect methods such as food rents? This chapter will also explore changes in animal sizes and the possible roles that the various domestic and wild species played in the economy of Ipswich. It concludes with some suggestions for further research.

II. Species Ratios

The large faunal assemblages from Middle Saxon, Late Saxon, and Early Medieval Ipswich all show that the Saxon and Early Medieval diet was based primarily on domestic mammals and birds. Hunting and fowling played only a minimal role in urban provisioning. The most common hunted mammals were red deer, followed by roe deer. Many of the red deer elements, especially in the Early Late Saxon collection, are fragments of antler that were used for the production of tools and ornaments. The Ipswich faunal assemblages lacked the diversity of wild birds that have been recovered from rural Anglo-Saxon sites in East Anglia. The paucity of wild avifauna also sets Ipswich apart from continental *emporia* such as Haithabu and Ribe. Many of the non-domestic bird remains recovered from Ipswich are corvids. These birds are most likely commensals, rather than elements of the early medieval diet.

The species ratios for the large domestic mammals from the Middle Saxon, Early Late Saxon, Middle Late Saxon, and Early Medieval assemblages from Ipswich are shown in Figure 6.1. The Early Late Saxon material from the St Nicholas Street site (4201) has been excluded from these calculations, since that deposit appears to be associated with specialised bone- and antler-working. The data reveal long-term continuities in animal provisioning at Ipswich. Cattle are always the most numerous species, followed by pigs and then caprines. The numbers of horse bones are very small throughout Ipswich's history, and there is no clear evidence in the form of butchery marks to indicate that horsemeat was part of the Late Saxon or Early Norman diet. A few butchery marks were recorded on the Middle Saxon horse remains. Poole's (2013, 327) study of hippophagy shows that butchered horse bones are common in Early and Middle Saxon rural sites, but only about half of the Late Saxon urban sites show evidence for horse butchery.

III. Cattle

Cattle would have been the primary source of meat for the inhabitants of Ipswich from the Middle Saxon through the Early Medieval period. This is unsurprising, since most of the early medieval sites in England and Northwest Europe appear to have been supplied with large quantities of beef. The age profiles for the Ipswich cattle show that its residents were supplied with both market-aged and older cattle (Fig. 6.2). The age classes used here follow Bourdillon and Coy (1977), see Crabtree (1990, 76).

Cattle and caprines may also have provided a variety of dairy products including milk, butter, and cheeses. Unfortunately, we have no clear evidence for dairying in the Ipswich archaeological record. In a specialised dairy

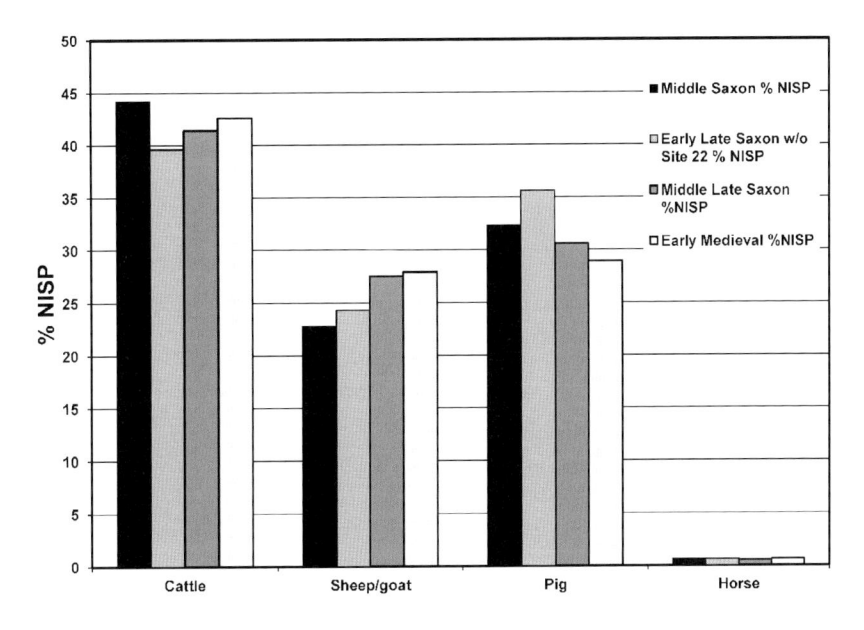

Figure 6.1 Species ratios for the large domestic mammals from Middle Saxon, Early Late Saxon, Middle Late Saxon and Early Medieval Ipswich

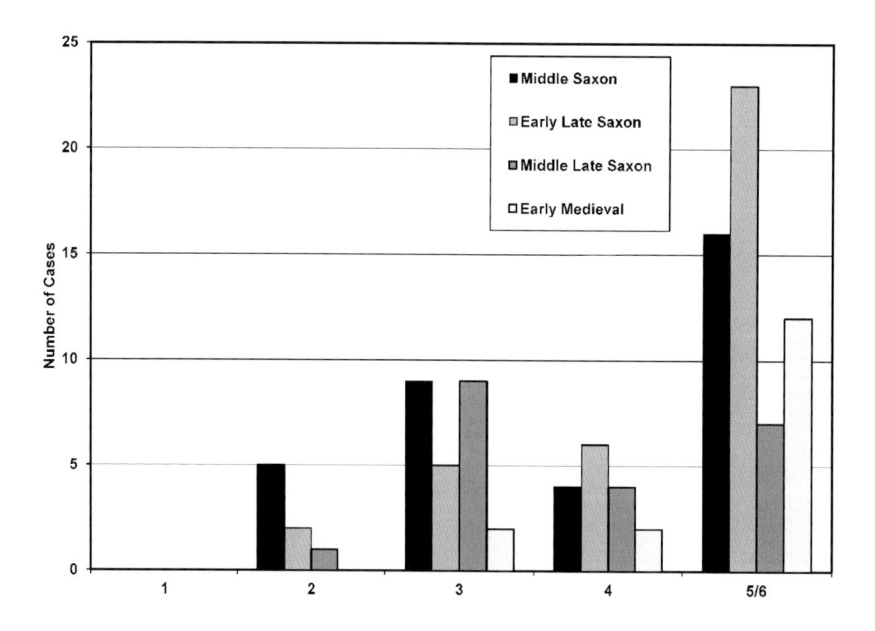

Figure 6.2 Age classes based on dental eruption and wear for cattle from Middle Saxon, Early Late Saxon, Middle Late Saxon and Early Medieval Ipswich

herd, we might expect to see the slaughter of excess calves, lambs and kids, and Coy's (2009) research on the fauna from the suburbs of Winchester showed that those Late Saxon assemblages included a substantial number of young calves. The age profiles for the cattle from all phases at Ipswich, on the other hand, are composed primarily of market-aged and older cattle.

Biometrical data suggest that the size of the Ipswich cattle decreased between AD 700 and 1150. This can be seen most clearly in the estimated withers heights (Fig. 5.3). As noted in Chapter 5, two factors are probably at play here. First, there is an apparent decline in the numbers of oxen that were sent to market. Sexing data suggest that more oxen are present in the Middle Saxon and Early Late Saxon assemblages than in the Middle Late Saxon and Early Medieval faunal collections (see also Crabtree 2017b). This factor alone, however, cannot explain all of the size decrease. It is also clear that the smallest of the Early Medieval cattle are smaller than their Middle Saxon counterparts, so we are probably seeing evidence for the kind of long-term size decrease that has been documented elsewhere (see, for example, Bökönyi 1971), although the timing of medieval size decrease varies by region. For example, the smallest medieval cattle in the Basque country of northern Spain were recovered from 8th- and 9th-century sites (Sirignano *et al.* 2014).

IV. Pigs

Pigs are always second in importance to cattle at Ipswich, and pork would have played a substantial role in the diet. The kill-patterns for the Saxon and Early Medieval pigs are what might be expected for a consumer assemblage. Most of the pigs are market-aged animals that were slaughtered in their second or third year of life. There are far fewer very young animals than are found in rural Anglo-Saxon assemblages (Crabtree 1990, 75–83). As a result of recent statistical research carried out by Evin *et al.* (2014) we can say with confidence that there are no wild boar remains in the Ipswich assemblages. The distribution of lower third molar lengths for all four phases at Ipswich is shown in Figure 6.3. All third molar lengths for the Ipswich pigs fall below 3.79mm, the cut-off that Evin *et al.* (2014) established as the upper limit for domestic pigs. Wild boars are exceptionally rare in medieval urban sites in Britain, but they are more common at early medieval urban sites on the Continent such as Antwerp (Crabtree *et al.* 2017).

V. Caprines

Sheep played a major role in the East Anglian economy throughout the Middle Ages, and they are the most numerous species at rural Anglo-Saxon sites such as Brandon and West Stow. They are consistently less numerous than cattle and pigs at Ipswich, although they do make up more than 20% of the identified large mammal bones throughout the Saxon and Early Medieval periods. This is striking given the proximity of Ipswich to the Sandlings region of East Anglia.

Osteometric data indicate that the Middle Saxon sheep from Ipswich are smaller than the Early Late Saxon and later sheep (see Fig. 3.7). They are comparable in size to the Middle Saxon sheep from rural sites like Brandon, and they are smaller than the sheep from late Roman Ipswich and Early Saxon West Stow. The question of why there are these small sheep in Middle Saxon East Anglia is one that deserves further attention in the future.

The mortality profiles for the sheep/goats from Ipswich are somewhat unspecialised, but they all include a substantial number of market-aged animals that were culled between 2 and 4 years of age (see Fig. 5.7). The faunal assemblages from all four chronological phases include both market-aged and older sheep. The Middle Saxon assemblage includes more first year culls of animals between 6 and 12 months of age, while the Late Saxon and Early Medieval assemblages include larger proportions of older animals. These are not the age profiles one would expect from specialised meat, milk, or wool production (Payne 1973), and they do not appear to

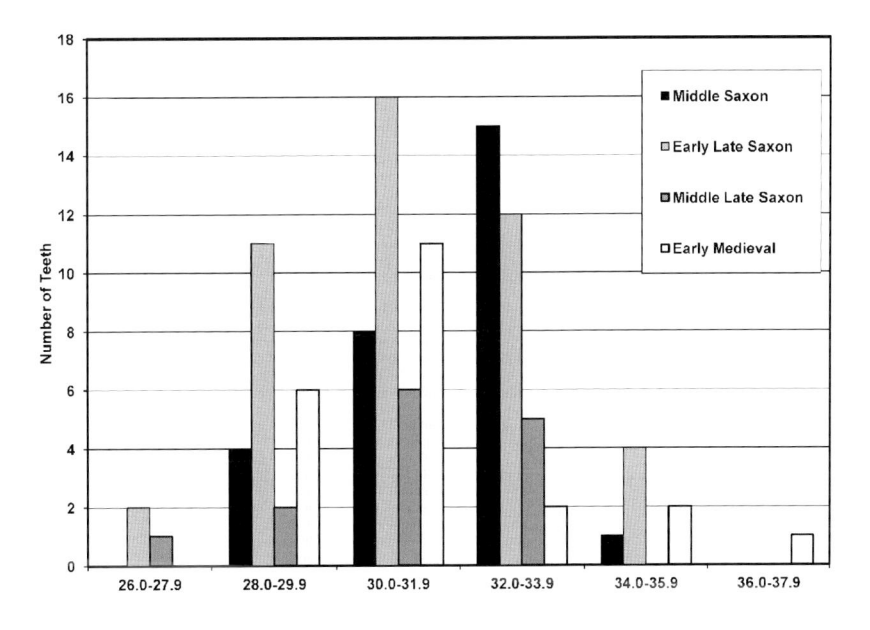

Figure 6.3 Lengths of the pig lower third molars from Middle Saxon, Early Late Saxon, Middle Late Saxon and Early Medieval sites from Ipswich

be ones that focused on herd security (Redding 1984). They appear to be consumer assemblages. The Middle Saxon assemblages include a larger number of first year culls that are animals which local farmers chose not to overwinter. The Late Saxon and Early Medieval assemblages are composed primarily of market-aged and adult animals, but they lack the elderly animals that are present on Anglo-Saxon rural sites.

VI. Horses

Horse bones are rare in the Ipswich assemblages; they generally make up only about 0.5% of the large domestic mammal remains. As noted above, there is no clear evidence to suggest that horses were part of the Ipswich diet after the Middle Saxon period. A small number of butchery marks were seen on the Middle Saxon horse remains from Ipswich, but there was no clear evidence for horse butchery in the Late Saxon and Early Medieval periods. In this respect, the horse remains from Ipswich are fundamentally different from those recovered from the Coppergate site in York. O'Connor (1989, 183–4) has argued that the horse bones from Coppergate appear to be butchered in the same way that the cattle bones were, and he suggests that they may have formed an occasional part of the Anglo-Scandinavian (Late Saxon) diet in York. While horses were not part of the Ipswich diet after the Middle Saxon period, the hides and bones may have had industrial uses, and the meat may have been fed to the dogs.

All the Ipswich horse remains belong to large ponies, generally between 13 and 14 hands (c. 130–140cm) in withers height. These ponies are similar in size to the horses depicted on the Bayeux Tapestry and they may well have been prestige items. They do not show the degree of pathologies that are seen on the 5th–6th-century working horses that were recovered from the Byzantine harbour in Istanbul (Onar et al. 2012). The Byzantine work and war horses were also generally larger than the horses from Ipswich; most were classified as either medium (withers heights of between 136 and 144cm) or large medium (withers heights between 144 and 152cm) (Onar et al. 2015), while the Ipswich horses were generally 140cm or less in withers height.

VII. Dogs

The dog remains from Ipswich have an interesting story to tell. Unfortunately, no complete dog bones were recovered from Middle Saxon Ipswich, but the dogs from Early and Middle Saxon rural sites in East Anglia tend to be large dogs with average withers heights of about 60cm (Crabtree 2015b). The Late Saxon and Early Medieval dogs from Ipswich show a much greater diversity in size, with estimated withers heights ranging from 28 to 56cm. Small and very small dogs were common in Roman Britain (see Baxter 2010), but they seem to disappear at the end of the Roman period. It is interesting to note that these smaller dogs reappear with the reappearance of towns, but the very small Roman lap dogs do not reappear in England until the early post-medieval period. The large dogs from rural Anglo-Saxon sites were probably herding and guard dogs, but the smaller dogs from Late Saxon and Early Medieval Ipswich may have served other functions as well. Some of the smaller dogs may have served as pets, and others may have been useful for catching rats and other vermin. The larger dogs may have guarded homes and workshops.

VIII. Poultry

Nearly all the bird remains recovered from Ipswich are the bones of domestic birds. The striking feature of the Ipswich avian assemblages is the extent to which domestic chickens outnumber domestic geese. At large Middle Saxon rural sites such as Brandon and Wicken Bonhunt, chickens outnumber geese by a factor of 3 to 2 (Crabtree 2012, 21, table 3.8). At Middle Saxon Ipswich, chickens outnumber geese by a ratio of nearly 4 to 1, and in the Early Medieval period, chickens outnumber geese by a ratio of more than 7 to 1. Bourdillon (2009) reports a similar pattern from the Late Saxon suburbs of Winchester.

It is probable that Anglo-Saxon and medieval chickens were kept primarily for their eggs, although they certainly ended up in the stew pot when their laying days were over. Traces of medullary bone are useful for identifying egg production, but this type of analysis was not conducted when the Ipswich animal bone assemblage was originally studied. Chickens may be far easier to keep in urban and suburban environments than geese are. In the United States, many urban and suburban families raised chickens during the Second World War. My in-laws kept chickens in their garage. This practice declined throughout the later 20th century, but a backyard chicken movement has developed in the past two decades (see Richardson 2017 for a sociological study of backyard chickens in San Diego, CA). My suburban New Jersey hometown now has a chicken ordinance that allows homeowners to keep chickens. Chickens have several advantages over geese in urban locations. In particular, they require less space, and they are better egg producers than geese are. Scientific and Cultural Perceptions on Human-Chicken Interactions (http://scicultchickens.org/about) is a multi-university project that studies the roles of chickens in human history. I have provided the investigators with the domestic chicken data from Brandon, and **will** do the same with the Ipswich chicken data.

IX. Urban Provisioning at Ipswich

One of the critical questions facing archaeologists is the issue of how the residents of Ipswich obtained meat and other animal products. Zeder (1989, see also Zeder 1991) developed two models for urban provisioning based on the studies of urbanism and state formation in the Ancient Near East. Zeder distinguished between direct provisioning — when urban residents obtain food directly from rural producers, and indirect provisioning — when urban residents are supplied with meat and other animal products and do not have that direct contact with producers. This question is critical to our understanding of the beginnings of urbanism since Bourdillon (1988, 1994) has developed an elegant model suggesting that the Middle Saxon inhabitants of Hamwic were provided with food indirectly through food rents. On the other hand, recent archaeological research has suggested that markets were well developed in Middle Saxon times in eastern England. As noted in previous chapters, while Jones (1993) argued that the development of markets in England was a response to the Viking invasions in the 9th century, increasing archaeological evidence for 'productive sites' and the use of coinage in the Middle Saxon period might indicate that some Middle Saxons obtained their meat through markets.

Zeder (1991, 37–42) identified some archaeological criteria that can be used to distinguish between direct and indirect provisioning at early urban sites. She argued that when urban residents are provisioned indirectly, archaeologists should expect to find limited diversity in the faunal assemblages. People who are provisioned indirectly receive a very limited number of species from a restricted set of age classes. Direct provisioning, on the other hand, should lead to a broader range of both animal species and age classes.

A cursory examination of the Ipswich Saxon and Early Medieval assemblages might suggest that the inhabitants of Ipswich had access to a restricted range of species. Very few hunted mammals and birds are present in the Ipswich assemblages. A closer look at the data might suggest otherwise. Throughout the history of Saxon and Medieval Ipswich, cattle, pigs and caprines are all relatively well represented in the faunal assemblages. While the rank order of the importance of the species remains unchanged, cattle, sheep/goats and pigs each make up at least 20% of all the Ipswich assemblages from the Middle Saxon through the Early Medieval period. In contrast, pigs make up only 10% of the Anglian/Middle Saxon faunal assemblage in York and only 15% of the faunal remains from Melbourne Street in Hamwic. The striking feature of the Ipswich assemblages is the evenness of the distribution of cattle, pigs and caprines. If the inhabitants of Ipswich had been indirectly provisioned through food rents, we would expect to see a much higher proportion of sheep in the Ipswich assemblages, since the Sandlings are prime sheep country. The age profiles from Saxon and Early Medieval Ipswich also include a broad range of market-aged and older animals, but they lack the very elderly animals that would be least attractive to buyers. While the zooarchaeological data from Ipswich are not a good match for Zeder's criteria, a plausible case for the direct provisioning of Ipswich from the Middle Saxon period onward can be made based on the overall species ratios and age profiles.

There is a second argument for direct provisioning through markets, and that is the long-term continuities in species ratios and age profiles that are apparent in the Ipswich data (see Crabtree 2016). There is no question that the Early Medieval inhabitants of Ipswich would have obtained meat and other food products through markets. The broad similarities in the faunal assemblages from all four phases of Ipswich suggest that this pattern was established in the Middle Saxon period.

The Ipswich faunal data also allow us to make an important point about the nature of the '*wic*' or *emporium* sites. There has been much archaeological and historical debate on the nature of these Middle Saxon sites and whether they represent the first true towns in post-Roman England (see, for example, Adams 2012). The long-term continuities in the provisioning of Ipswich from the Middle Saxon through the Early Medieval period certainly provide support for the idea that the *emporia* do, in fact, represent Middle Saxon urbanism.

X. Future Directions

The animal bone remains from Ipswich were initially identified by Patricia Stevens and Don Bramwell between 1985 and 1990. I became involved with the project in the early 1990s, and I had completed my initial research and draft publications by 1994. For a variety of different reasons, our research was not published in a timely manner.

Today we have a variety of new analytical methods for the study of animal bones that were not available to us 25 years ago, and I would like to suggest some possible avenues for research. Future isotopic research may allow us to answer some questions. One of the critical ones is the question of where the Ipswich pigs were actually reared. Were they raised in the town and fed human refuse, or were they put out to pannage in more rural wooded areas? Hammond and O'Connor (2013) used stable carbon and nitrogen isotopes to answer similar questions about pigs from medieval York. Strontium isotope analyses may allow archaeologists to identify whether the pigs that were consumed in Ipswich were brought in from regions that are remote from eastern Suffolk.

More detailed biometrical studies may also yield interesting results. Are the small Middle Saxon sheep unique to Suffolk, or can we identify them in other parts of Anglo-Saxon England? Is there more widespread evidence for size decrease in cattle during later Saxon and medieval times? In order to carry out more detailed biometrical studies, we need large and well-dated assemblages that have been carefully collected and curated. As Holmes (2014) has suggested, we need access to individual measurements and not just ranges and means. This means that zooarchaeologists need to publish their original data and not just their animal bone reports.

Finally, well-designed aDNA studies have great potential to identify characteristics of faunal assemblages that cannot be studied using conventional zooarchaeological techniques (see, for example, Campana *et al.* 2013). For example, recent genetic studies have shown that spotted horses became less popular during the Middle Ages (Wutke *et al.* 2016).

While there are many possible directions that the research on animal bone remains could take in future, this volume presents the foundational data on bone identifications, species ratios, age profiles, and measurement data. The value of the Ipswich data is that archaeological research carried out between 1974 and 1990 allows both archaeologists and archaeozoologists to trace the history of urban provisioning at Ipswich from the 7th century to 1150. The Ipswich faunal assemblages are unique in that they provide a continuous record of urban provisioning from the rise of the *emporia* in the 7th and 8th centuries through to the early Norman period.

Appendix. Faunal remains from other periods in Ipswich, and amphibian remains

	NISP
Domestic mammals	
Cattle (*Bos taurus*)	302
Goat (*Capra hircus*)	1
Sheep/goat	50
Pig (*Sus scrofa*)	107
Horse (*Equus caballus*)	6
Dog (*Canis familiaris*)	1
Wild mammals	
Red deer (*Cervus elaphus*)	1
Roe deer (*Capreolus capreolus*)	5
Domestic birds	
Domestic fowl (*Gallus gallus*)	10
Total NISP	483

Table A.1 Species list for St Peter's Street Ipswich (5203) Early Middle Saxon

	NISP
Domestic mammals	
Cattle (*Bos taurus*)	29
Sheep/goat	12
Pig (*Sus scrofa*)	24
Horse (*Equus caballus*)	1
Dog (*Canis familiaris*)	1
Cat (*Felis catus*)	2
Wild mammals	
Hare (*Lepus* sp.)	1
Domestic birds	
Domestic fowl (*Gallus gallus*)	5
Domestic goose (*Anser anser*)	1
Total NISP	76

Table A.3 Species list for Tower Ramparts Ipswich (0802) Late Medieval

	NISP
Domestic mammals	
Cattle (*Bos taurus*)	36
Sheep (*Ovis aries*)	2
Goat (*Capra hircus*)	2
Sheep/goat	46
Pig (*Sus scrofa*)	26
Horse (*Equus caballus*)	23
Dog (*Canis familiaris*)	2
Cat (*Felis catus*)	1
Total NISP	138

Table A.2 Species list for Foundation Street/Wingfield Ipswich (4601) Middle Saxon/Early Late Saxon

	NISP
Domestic mammals	
Cattle (*Bos taurus*)	193
Sheep (*Ovis aries*)	3
Goat (*Capra hircus*)	32
Sheep/goat	270
Pig (*Sus scrofa*)	129
Horse (*Equus caballus*)	6
Dog (*Canis familiaris*)	4
Cat (*Felis catus*)	5
Wild mammals	
Red deer (*Cervus elaphus*)	1
Hare (*Lepus* sp.)	3
Domestic birds	
Domestic fowl (*Gallus gallus*)	41
Domestic goose (*Anser anser*)	7
Total NISP	694

Table A.4 Species list for Bridge Street Ipswich (6202) Late Medieval

	NISP
Domestic mammals	
Cattle (*Bos taurus*)	16
Sheep (*Ovis aries*)	1
Goat (*Capra hircus*)	52
Sheep/goat	28
Pig (*Sus scrofa*)	4
Horse (*Equus caballus*)	3
Domestic birds	
Domestic fowl (*Gallus gallus*)	2
Total NISP	106

Table A.5 Species list for St George's Street Ipswich (9802) Late Medieval

	NISP
Domestic mammals	
Cattle (*Bos taurus*)	28
Sheep (*Ovis aries*)	3
Sheep/goat	18
Pig (*Sus scrofa*)	73
Horse (*Equus caballus*)	1
Domestic birds	
Domestic fowl (*Gallus gallus*)	5
Total NISP	128

Table A.6 Species list for Foundation Street/Wingfield Ipswich (4601) Late Medieval

	NISP
Domestic mammals	
Cattle (*Bos taurus*)	1
Sheep/goat	3
Pig (*Sus scrofa*)	3
Dog (*Canis familiaris*)	1
Wild mammals	
Hare (*Lepus* sp.)	7
Domestic birds	
Domestic fowl (*Gallus gallus*)	5
Domestic goose (*Anser anser*)	4
Wild birds	
Starling (*Sturnus vulgaris*)	1
Total NISP	25

Table A.7 Species list for Tower Ramparts Ipswich (0802) Late Medieval/Early Post-Medieval

	NISP
Domestic mammals	
Cattle (*Bos taurus*)	27
Sheep/goat	83
Pig (*Sus scrofa*)	41
Horse (*Equus caballus*)	3
Wild mammals	
Red deer (*Cervus elaphus*)	1
Roe deer (*Capreolus capreolus*)	1
Hare (*Lepus* sp.)	1
Domestic birds	
Domestic fowl (*Gallus gallus*)	13
Domestic goose (*Anser anser*)	1
Total NISP	171

Table A.8 Species list for Bridge Street Ipswich (6202) Late Medieval/Early Post-Medieval

	NISP
Domestic mammals	
Cattle (*Bos taurus*)	26
Sheep/goat	19
Pig (*Sus scrofa*)	11
Wild mammals	
Rabbit (*Oryctolagus cunniculus*)	4
Domestic birds	
Domestic fowl (*Gallus gallus*)	2
Domestic goose (*Anser anser*)	3
Total NISP	65

Table A.9 Species list for Bridge Street Ipswich (6202) Post-Medieval

Sites	Frog (*Rana* sp.)	Frog/Toad
Middle Saxon		
6202		1
6904	62	
Early Late Saxon		
0802		32
4301	11	1
4801		3
Middle Late Saxon		
4201		10
Early Medieval		
4201	1	
4601	1	1

Table A10 Amphibian remains from Saxon and Medieval contexts at Ipswich

Bibliography

Adams, C., 2012 — 'Economic collapse? A historical and archaeological perspective on the Anglo-Saxon emporium,' *Primary Source* 2 (2), 1–8. Available: https://psource.sitehost.iu.edu/PDF/Archive%20Articles/Spring2012/2012%20-%20Spring%20-%201%20-%20Adams,%20Claire.pdf Accessed 29 October 2020

Albarella, U. and Thomas, R., 2002 — 'They dined on crane: Bird consumption, wild fowling and status in Medieval England,' *Acta Zoologica Cracoviensia* 45, 23–28

Andrews, P., 1997 — *Excavations at Hamwic, Volume 2: Excavations at Six Dials*, Counc. Brit. Archaeol. Res. Rep. 109 (London: Council for British Archaeology)

Ayers, B., 2011 — 'The growth of an urban landscape: recent research in early medieval Norwich', *Early Medieval Europe* 19, 62–90

Bartosiewicz, L., Van Neer, W., and Lentacker, A., 1997 — *Draught Cattle: Their Osteological Identification and History*, (Tervuren: Musée Royale de l'Afrique Centrale)

Baxter I.L., 2010 — 'Small Roman dogs,' available online at: http://alexandriaarchive.org/bonecommons/archive/files/baxter_2010_small_roman_dogs_6dc7d64928.pdf

Becker, C. and Grupe, G., 2012 — 'Archaeometry meets archaeozoology: Viking Hedeby and medieval Schleswig reconsidered,' *Archaeol. Anthropol. Sci.* 4, 241–262

Bellens, T., Schryvers, A., Tys, D., Termote, D., Nakken, H., 2012 — 'Archeologisch onderzoek van de Antwerpse burcht,' *Monumenten en Landschappen* 31 (1), 4–21

Biddle, M., 1975 — 'Excavations at Winchester, 1971: Tenth and Final Interim Report Part II,' *Antiquaries Journal* 55 (2), 295–337

Biddle, M., 1984 — 'London on the Strand,' *Popular Archaeology* 6 (1), 23–27

Biddle, M., 1990 — 'Albert Ricket Archaeological Trust Lecture. The study of Winchester: Archaeology and history in a British town, 1961–1983', in E.G. Stanley (ed.), *British Academy Papers on Anglo-Saxon England*, 299–341 (Oxford: Oxford University Press)

Biddle, M. and Hill, D., 1971 — 'Late Saxon planned towns,' *Antiquaries Journal* 71, 70–85

Blinkhorn, P., 1999 — 'Of cabbages and kings: production, trade and consumption in Middle Saxon England,' in M. Anderton (ed.), *Anglo-Saxon Trading Centres and Their Hinterlands: Beyond the Emporia*, 4–23 (Glasgow: Cruithne Press)

Blinkhorn, P., 2012 — *The Ipswich Ware Project: Ceramics, Trade and Society in Middle Saxon England*, Medieval Pottery Research Group Occasional Paper 7 (Dorchester)

Boessneck, J., 1969 — 'Osteological differences between sheep (*Ovis aries* Linné) and goat (*Capra hircus* Linné),' in D. Brothwell and E. Higgs (eds), *Science in Archaeology*, 331–358 (London: Thames and Hudson)

Boessneck, J.A., Müller, H.-H. and Tiechert, M., 1964 — 'Osteologische Unterschneidungsmerkmale zwischen Schaf (*Ovis aries* Linné) und Ziege (*Capra hircus* Linné)', *Kühn-Archiv* 78, 1–129

Bökönyi, S., 1971 — 'The development and history of domestic animals in Hungary: The Neolithic through the Middle Ages,' *American Anthropologist* 73, 640–674

Bourdillon, J., 1988 — 'Countryside and town: the animal resources of Saxon Southampton,' in Della Hooke (ed.), *Anglo-Saxon Settlements*, 177–195 (Oxford: Blackwell)

Bourdillon, J., 1994 — 'The animal provisioning of Saxon Southampton,' in J. Rackham (ed.) *Environment and Economy in Anglo-Saxon England*, Counc. Brit. Archaeol. Res. Rep. 89, 120–125 (London: Council for British Archaeology)

Bourdillon, J., 2009 — 'Late Saxon animal bone from the northern and eastern suburbs and the city defenses,' in D. Serjeantson and H. Rees (eds), *Food, Craft and Status in Medieval Winchester: The plant and animal remains from the suburbs and the city defences*, Winchester Excavations Volume 10, 55–81 (Winchester: Winchester Museums)

Bourdillon, J. and Coy, J., 1977 — *Statistical appendix to accompany the animal bone report on material from Melbourne Street (Sites I, IV, V, VI, and XX) excavated by the Southampton Archaeological Research Committee between 1971 and 1976*, Manuscript available from Southampton Archaeological Research Council

Bourdillon, J., and Coy, J., 1980 — 'The animal bones,' in P. Holdsworth, *Excavations at Melbourne Street, Southampton, 1971–76*, Counc. Brit. Archaeol. Res. Rep. 33, 79–121 (London: Council for British Archaeology)

Brisbane, M.A., 1994 — '*Hamwic* (Saxon Southampton): the origin and development of an eighth century port and production centre,' Actes des congrès de la Société d'archéologie médiévale 4 (1), 27–34

British Ornithologists' Union, 1971 — *The Status of Birds in Britain and Ireland*, (Oxford: Blackwell)

Brown, R., Teague, S., Loe, L., Sudds, B. and Popescu, E., 2020 — *Excavations at Stoke Quay, Ipswich: southern Gypeswic and the parish of St Augustine*, East Anglian Archaeology 172 (Oxford and London: Oxford Archaeology and Pre-Construct Archaeology)

Campana, D.V., 2010 — *FAUNA: Database and analysis software for faunal analysis*, Poster presented at the meeting of the International Council for Archaeozoology, Paris, August 2010

Campana, M.G., Bower, M.A. and Crabtree, P.J., 2013 — 'Ancient DNA for the Archaeologist: the Future of African Research,' *African Archaeological Review* 30, 21–37

Carver, M.O.H., 2005 — *Sutton Hoo: a Seventh-Century Princely Burial Ground and Its Context*, Rep. Res. Comm. Soc. Antiq. London 69 (London: British Museum Press)

Coupland, S., 2002 — 'Trading places: Quentovic and Dorestad reassessed,' *Early Medieval Europe* 11 (3), 209–232

Cowie, R., Blackmore, L., Davis, A., Keily, J. and Rielly, K., 2012 — *Lundenwic: Excavations in Middle Saxon London, 1987–2000*, MoLA Monograph 63 (London: Museum of London Archaeology)

Coy, J., 2009	'Late Saxon and medieval animal bone from the western suburb,' in D. Serjeantson and H. Rees (eds), *Food, Craft and Status in Medieval Winchester: The plant and animal remains from the suburbs and the city defenses*, Winchester Excavations Volume 10, 27–54 (Winchester: Winchester Museums)	Crabtree, P.J., 2018	*Early Medieval Britain — The Rebirth of Towns in the Post-Roman West* (Cambridge: Cambridge University Press)
		Crabtree, P.J. and Campana, D.V., 2012	'Traces of butchery and bone working,' in B. Adams and P. Crabtree, *Comparative Osteology: A Laboratory and Field Guide to Common North American Animals*, 407–28 (Waltham, MA: Academic Press)
Coy, J.P. and Maltby, M., 1991	'The animal bone analyses on the M3 project — a review,' in Fasham, P.J. and Whinney, R.J.B., (eds) *Archaeology and the M3: the Watching Brief, the Anglo-Saxon Settlement at Abbots Worthy and Retrospective Sections*, Hampshire Field Club and Archaeological Society Monograph 7, 97–104	Crabtree, P.J. and Campana, D.V., 2014	'Animal bone,' in A. Tester, S. Anderson, I. Riddler and R. Carr *Brandon, Staunch Meadow, Suffolk: A High Status Middle Saxon Settlement on the Fen Edge*, East Anglian Archaeology 151, 296–312 (Bury St Edmunds: Suffolk County Council Archaeological Service)
Crabtree, P.J., 1982	*Early Anglo-Saxon Animal Economy: An Analysis of the Animal Bone Remains from the Early Saxon Site of West Stow, Suffolk*, Unpublished PhD dissertation, University of Pennsylvania	Crabtree, P.J. and Campana, D.V., 2015	'Wool production, wealth, and trade in Middle Saxon England,' in B.S. Arbuckle and S.A. McCarty (eds), *Animals and Inequality in the Ancient World*, 337–353 (Boulder: University of Colorado Press)
Crabtree, P.J., 1990	*West Stow: Early Anglo-Saxon Animal Husbandry*, East Anglian Archaeology 47 (Ipswich: Suffolk County Planning Department)	Crabtree, P.J. and Campana, D.V., 2017	'Where are our goats?' in J. Lev-Tov, A. Gilbert and P. Hesse (eds) *The Wide Lens in Archaeology: Honoring Brian Hesse's Contributions to Anthropological Archaeology*, 389–399 (Atlanta: Lockwood)
Crabtree, P.J., 2007	'Animals as Material Culture in Middle Saxon England: The Zooarchaeological Evidence for Wool Production at Brandon,' in A. Pluskowski (ed.), *Breaking and Shaping Beastly Bodies: Animals as Material Culture in the Middle Ages*, 161–169 (Oxford: Oxbow Press)		
		Crabtree, P.J., Reilly, E., Wouters, P., Devos, Y., Bellens, T. and Schryvers, A., 2017	'Environmental Evidence from Early Urban Antwerp: New Data from Archaeology, Micromorphology, Macrofauna and Insect Remains', *Quaternary International* 460, 107–123
Crabtree, P.J., 2012	*Middle Saxon Animal Husbandry in East Anglia*, East Anglian Archaeology 143 (Bury St Edmunds: Suffolk County Council Archaeological Service)		
		Crabtree, P.J. and Stevens, P.M., 1994	'The animal bones from Ipswich: Report for publication,' available: http://archaeologydataservice.ac.uk/archiveDS/archiveDownload?t=arch-1644-1/dissemination/pdf/Reports_General/IAS_animalbone_Crabtree_R187_publication.pdf (This version is text only. It includes none of the data tables or graphics that were in the original report)
Crabtree, P., 2013	'West Stow West Zooarchaeology Data', from *West Stow West Zooarchaeology*. Edited or directed by P. Crabtree. Released: 2013-06-05. Open Context. <http://opencontext.org/tables/1bd7c10da9c0b35c70b2c6a86276e617> DOI: https://doi.org/10.6078/M7W66HPZ Accessed 29 October 2020		
		Dallas, C., 1993	*Excavations in Thetford by B.K. Davison between 1964 and 1970*, East Anglian Archaeology 62 (Dereham: Norfolk Museums Service)
Crabtree, P., 2014	'Animal husbandry and farming in East Anglia from the 5th to the 10th centuries CE,' *Quaternary International* 346, 102–108	Dobney, K., Jacques, D., Barrett, J. and Johnstone, C., 2007	*Farmers, Monks and Aristocrats: The Environmental Archaeology of Anglo-Saxon Flixborough*, Excavations at Flixborough Vol 3 (Oxford: Oxbow Books)
Crabtree, P.J., 2015a	'Urban-Rural Interactions in East Anglia: the Evidence from Zooarchaeology,' in Alexis Wilkin, John Naylor, Derek Keene and Arnoud-Jan Bijsterveld (eds) *Dynamic Interactions: Town and Countryside in Northwestern Europe in the Middle Ages*, The Medieval Countryside 11, 35–48 (Turnhout, Belgium: Brepols)		
		Ervynck, A., Van Neer, W., Hüster-Plogmann, H. and Schibler, J., 2003	'Beyond affluence: the zooarchaeology of luxury,' *World Archaeology* 34 (3), 428–441
Crabtree, P.J., 2015b	'A note on the role of dogs in Anglo-Saxon society: evidence from East Anglia,' *International Journal of Osteoarchaeology* 25 (6), 976–980	Essig, M., 2015	*Lesser Beasts: The Snout-to-Tail History of the Humble Pig* (New York: Basic Books)
Crabtree, P.J., 2016	'Zooarchaeology at Medieval Ipswich: from '*wic*' to regional market town,' in Ben Jervis, Lee Broderick and Idoia Grau-Sologestoa (eds), *Objects, Environment and Everyday Life in Medieval Europe*, 19–39 (Turnhout, Belgium: Brepols)	Evin, A., Cicchi, T., Escarguel, G., Owen, J., Larsen, G., Vidarsdottir, V.S. and Dobney, K., 2014	'Using traditional biometrical data to distinguish between west Paleoarctic wild boar and domestic pigs in the archaeological record: new methods and standards,' *Journal of Archaeological Science* 43, 1–8
Crabtree, P.J., 2017a	'State formation in Anglo-Saxon England,' in P. Crabtree and P. Bogucki, (eds), *European Archaeology as Anthropology: Essays in Memory of Bernard Wailes*, 245–259 (Philadelphia: University of Pennsylvania Museum)	Fern C., 2015	*Before Sutton Hoo: the prehistoric remains and Early Anglo-Saxon Cemetery at Tranmer House, Bromeswell, Suffolk*, East Anglian Archaeology 155 (Bury St Edmunds: Suffolk County Council)
Crabtree, P.J., 2017b	'The diet of Ipswich from the Middle Saxon through the Medieval Periods,' in Alice Choyke and Gerhard Jaritz (eds), *Animaltown: Beasts in Medieval Urban Space*, BAR International Series 2858, 35–40 (Oxford: BAR Publishing)	Friedman, J. and Rowlands, M.J., 1977	'Notes toward an epigenetic model of the evolution of civilization,' in J. Friedman and M.J. Rowlands (eds), *The Evolution of Social Systems*, 201–76 (London: Duckworth)

Gardiner, M. 1997 — 'The exploitation of sea-mammals in Medieval England: bones and their social context' *Archaeological Journal* 154 (1), 173–195

Grant, A., 1976 — 'The use of tooth wear as a guide to the age of domestic animals,' in B. Cunliffe (ed.), *Excavations at Portchester Castle, Vol. II: Saxon*, Rep. Res. Comm. Soc. Antiq. London 33, 245–79 (London: Society of Antiquaries)

Grant, A., 1982 — 'The use of tooth wear as a guide to the age of domestic ungulates,' in B. Wilson, C. Grigson, and S. Payne (eds) *Ageing and Sexing Animal Bones from Archaeological Sites*, BAR British Series 109, 91–108 (Oxford: British Archaeological Reports)

Halstead, P., Collins, P. and Isaakidou, V., 2002 — 'Sorting the Sheep from the Goats: Morphological Distinctions between the Mandibles and Mandibular Teeth of Adult *Ovis* and *Capra*,' *Journal of Archaeological Science* 29, 545–553

Hall, R., 1984 — *The Excavations at York: the Viking Dig* (London: The Bodley Head)

Hall, R., 1994 — *Viking Age York* (London: Batsford)

Hall, R.A., with Evans, D.T., Hunter-Mann, K. and Mainman, A.J., 2014 — *Anglo-Scandinavian Occupation at 16–22 Coppergate*, Archaeology of York 8/5 (York: Council for British Archaeology for the York Archaeological Trust)

Hamerow, H., 2007 — 'Agrarian production and the emporia of mid Saxon England, ca. 650–850,' in J. Henning (ed.), *Post-Roman Towns, Trade and Settlement in Europe and Byzantum, Vol. 1: The Heirs of the Roman West* (Berlin: Walter de Gruyter)

Hammon, A., 2011 — 'Understanding the Romano-British–Early Medieval Transition: A Zooarchaeological Perspective from Wroxeter (*Viroconium Cornoviorum*),' *Britannia* 42, 275–305

Hammond, C. and O'Connor, T., 2013 — 'Pig diet in medieval York: carbon and nitrogen stable isotopes,' *Archaeol. Anthropol. Sci.* 5, 123–127

Hansen, I. and Wickham, C., (eds), 2000 — *The Long Eighth Century: Production, distribution and demand* (Leiden: Brill)

Hatting, T., 1991 — 'The archaeozoology, in M. Bencard, L.B, Jørgensen, and H.B. Madsen, (eds), *Ribe Excavations 1970–76, Vol. 3*, 43–57 (Aarhus: Universiteitsforlag)

Hodges, R., 1982 — *Dark Age Economics: The origins of towns and trade AD 600–1000*, (London: Duckworth)

Hodges, R., 1989 — *Dark Age Economics: The origins of towns and trade AD 600–1000*, second edition (London: Duckworth)

Hodges, R. 2012 — *Dark Age Economics: A new audit* (London: Duckworth)

Holdsworth, P., 1980 — *Excavations at Melbourne Street, Southampton, 1971–76*, Counc. Brit. Archaeol. Res. Rep. 33 (London: Council for British Archaeology)

Holmes, M., 2014 — 'Changes in the size and shape of animals throughout the English Saxon period,' *Journal of Archaeological Science* 43, 77–90

Howard, M., 1963 — 'An assessment of a prehistoric technique of bovine husbandry', in A.E. Mournat and F.E. Zeuner (eds), *Man and Cattle*, Royal Anthropological Institute Occasional Paper 18, 92–100

Hurst, J.J., and West, S.E., 1957 — 'Saxo-Norman pottery in East Anglia. Part II. Thetford ware with an account of Middle Saxon Ipswich ware,' *Proceedings of the Cambridge Antiquarian Society* 50, 29–60

Jones, A.K.G., 1979 — 'Fish bones,' *Ipswich 1974–90 Excavation Archive*. SCCAS unpublished archive report. Available: http://archaeologydataservice.ac.uk/archiveDS/archiveDownload?t=arch-1644-1/dissemination/pdf/Reports_General/IAS_fishbone_R166.pdf. Accessed 29 October 2020

Jones, G., 1984 — 'Animal bones,' in A. Rogerson and C. Dallas (eds), *Excavations in Thetford 1948–59 and 1973–80*, East Anglian Archaeology 22, 187–192 (Dereham: Norfolk Archaeological Unit)

Jones, R.T., 1976 — *Computer based osteometric archaeozoology*, Ancient Monuments Laboratory Report 2333

Jones, R.T. and Serjeantson, D., 1983 — *The animal bones from five sites at Ipswich*, Ancient Monuments Laboratory Report 3951. Available: https://research.historicengland.org.uk/PrintReport.aspx?i=2471&ru=%2FResults.aspx%3Fp%3D496. Accessed 29 October 2020

Jones, S.R.H., 1993 — 'Transaction costs, institutional change, and the emergence of a market economy in later Anglo-Saxon England,' *The Economic History Review*, New Series 46 (4), 658–678

Jørgensen, D., 2013 — 'Pigs and pollards: Medieval insights into UK pasture restoration,' *Sustainability* 5, 387–399

Kemp, B., 1996 — *Anglian Settlement at 46–52 Fishergate*, The Archaeology of York 7/1, (London: Council for British Archaeology)

King, A.C., 1984 — 'Animal bones and the dietary identity of military and civilian groups in Roman Britain, Germany and Gaul,' in T. Blagg and A. King (eds), *Military and Civilian in Roman Britain*, BAR British Series 137, 187–217 (Oxford: British Archaeological Reports)

King, A.C., 1999 — 'Animals and the Roman army: the evidence of animal bones,' in A. Goldsworthy and I. Haynes (eds), 'The Roman Army as a Community,' *Journal of Roman Archaeology* Supplementary Series 34, 139–149

Locker, A. and Jones, A., 1983 — 'Ipswich — The Fish Remains (from sites 0802, 1804, 3410, 5202, 5801, 5901, 5902, 6202, 6904 & 7404), *Ipswich 1974–90 Excavation Archive*. SCCAS unpublished archive report. Available: http://archaeologydataservice.ac.uk/archiveDS/archiveDownload?t=arch-1644-1/dissemination/pdf/Reports_General/IAS_fishbones.pdf. Accessed 29 October 2020

Loveluck, C. and Tys, D., 2006 — 'Coastal societies, exchange and identity along the Channel and southern North Sea shores of Europe, AD 600–1000,' *Journal of Maritime Archaeology* 1, 140–169

Lyman, L., 2008 — *Quantitative Paleozoology* (Cambridge: Cambridge University Press)

Malcolm, G. and Bowsher, D. with Cowie R., 2003 — *Middle Saxon London: Excavations at the Royal Opera House 1989–99*, MoLAS Monograph 15 (London: Museum of London Archaeology Service)

Marzluff, J.M. and Angell, T., 2005 — *In the Company of Crows and Ravens*, (New Haven, Connecticut: Yale University Press)

Milne, C. and Crabtree, P., 2002 — 'Revealing Meals: Ethnicity, Economic Status and Diet at Five Points, 1800–1860,' in Rebecca Yamin (ed.), *Tales of the Five Points: Working Class Life in Nineteenth Century New York*.

Moreland, J., 2001 — Volume II: An Interpretive Approach to Working Class Life, 130–196 (New York: General Services Administration)

Moreland, J., 2001 — 'Emporia', in P. Crabtree (ed.) *Medieval Archaeology: An encyclopedia*, 92–97 (New York: Garland)

Naismith, R., 2012 — *Money and Power in Anglo-Saxon England: The Southern English Kingdoms 757–865* (Cambridge: Cambridge University Press)

O'Connor, T., 1982 — *Animal Bones from Flaxengate, Lincoln, c. 870–1500*, Archaeology of Lincoln 18/1, (Council for British Archaeology, for Lincolnshire Archaeological Trust)

O'Connor, T.P., 1989 — *Bones from Anglo-Scandinavian Levels at 16–22 Coppergate*, The Archaeology of York 15/3, (London: Council for British Archaeology)

O'Connor, T.P., 1991 — *Bones from 46–54 Fishergate*, The Archaeology of York 15/4, (London: Council for British Archaeology)

O'Connor, T.P., 2012 — 'Animal husbandry,' in H. Hamerow, D.A. Hinton and S. Crawford, (eds), *The Oxford Handbook of Anglo-Saxon Archaeology*, 361–376 (Oxford: Oxford University Press)

Onar, V., Alpak, H., Armutak, A. and Chroszcz, A., 2012 — 'Byzantine horse skeletons of Theodosius Harbour 1. Paleopathology,' *Revue Méd. Vét.* 163, 139–146

Onar, V., Pazvent, G., Armutak, A. and Alpak, H., 2015 — 'Byzantine horse skeletons of Theodosius Harbour 2. Withers height estimation,' *Revue Méd. Vét.* 166, 30–42

Payne, S., 1973 — 'Kill-off patterns in sheep and goats: the mandibles from Asvan Kale', *Anatolian Studies* 23, 281–303

Pestell, T. and Ulmschneider, K. (eds), 2003 — *Markets in Early Medieval Europe: Trading and 'Productive' Sites, 650–850* (Macclesfield, UK: Windgather Press)

Pirenne, H., 1925 (1969) — *Medieval Cities: Their Origins and the Revival of Trade* (Princeton, NJ: Princeton University Press)

Plogmann, H.H., 2006 — 'Untersuchungen an den Skelettresten von Säugtieren und Vögeln aus dem Hafen von Haithabu,' in K. Schietzel (ed.) *Berichte über dir Ausgrabigen in Haithabu* 35, 25–125 (Neumünster: Wachholtz Verlag)

Poole, K., 2013 — 'Horses for courses? Religious change and dietary shifts in Anglo-Saxon England,' *Oxford Journal of Archaeology* 32, 319–333

Prummel, W., 1983 — *Excavations at Dorestad 2: Early Medieval Dorestad an Archaeozoological Study* (Amersfoort: ROB)

Redding, R., 1984 — 'Theoretical determinants of a herder's decisions: Modeling variations in the sheep/goat ratio', in J. Clutton-Brock and C. Grigson (eds) *Animals and Archaeology 3: Herders and Their Flocks*, BAR International Series 202, 223–241 (Oxford: British Archaeological Reports)

Reichstein, H. and Tiessen, M., 1974 — 'Materialen zur Kenntnis der Hausetiere Haithabus,' *Berichte über Ausgrabungen in Haithabu* 7, 9–101

Richardson, J., 2017 — *Beyond distinction: the complex motivations of backyard chicken keepers*, Unpublished MS Thesis, Department of Sociology, University of Wisconsin-Madison

Rielly, K., 2003 — 'The animal and fish bone,' in G. Malcolm, D. Bowsher and R. Cowie, *Middle Saxon London: Excavations at the Royal Opera House, 1989–99*, MoLAS Monograph 15, 315–324 (London: Museum of London Archaeology Service)

Rizzetto, M., Crabtree, P. and Albarella, U., 2017 — 'Livestock changes at the beginning and end of the Roman period in Britain: issues of acculturation, adaptation and 'improvement',' *European Journal of Archaeology* 20 (3), 535–556

Rogerson, A. and Dallas, C. (eds), 1984 — *Excavations in Thetford 1948–59 and 1973–80*, East Anglian Archaeology 22, 187–192 (Dereham: Norfolk Archaeological Unit)

Royal Society for the Protection of Birds, 2009 — *Cranes return to East Anglian Fens*. Available: http://www.rspb.org.uk/our-work/rspb-news/news/details.aspx?id=tcm:9-222807. Accessed 29 October 2020

Scull, C., 2009 — *Early Medieval (late 5th–early 8th centuries AD) Cemeteries at Boss Hall and Buttermarket, Ipswich, Suffolk*, Society for Medieval Archaeology Monograph 27 (London: Society for Medieval Archaeology)

Scull, C., Minter, F. and Plouviez, J., 2016 — 'Social and economic complexity in early medieval England: a central place complex of the East Anglian kingdom at Rendlesham, Suffolk,' *Antiquity* 90 (354), 1594–1612

Seetah, K., 2018 — *Humans, Animals and the Craft of Slaughter in Archaeo-Historic Societies*, (Cambridge: Cambridge University Press)

Serjeantson, D. and Crabtree, P. with J. Mulville, K. Ayres, Claire I. and A. Locker, 2018 — 'How Pious? How Wealthy? The Status of Eynsham and St Albans Abbeys Between the 8th and the 12th Centuries Re-examined in Light of their Food Consumption', in B. Jervis (ed.) *The Middle Ages Revisited: Studies in the Archaeology and History of Medieval Southern England Presented to Professor David A. Hinton*, 115–140 (Oxford: Archaeopress)

Silver, I.A., 1969 — 'The ageing of domestic animals', in D. Brothwell and E. Higgs (eds), *Science in Archaeology*, 283–302 (London: Thames and Hudson)

Sirignano, C., Sologestoa, I.G., Ricci, P., García-Collado, M.I., Altieri, S., Quirós Castillo, J.A. and Lubritto, C., 2014 — 'Animal husbandry during Early and High Middle Ages in the Basque Country (Spain),' *Quaternary International* 346, 138–148

Solti, B., 1985 — 'Vergleichende osteometrische Untersuchungen uber den Korperbau europaischer Grossfalken sowie dessen funktionelle Beziehungen', *Folio Historico Naturalia Musei Matraensis* 10, 115–30

Stoodley, N., 2002 — 'The origins of *Hamwic* and its central role in the seventh century as revealed by recent archaeological discoveries,' in B. Hårdh and L. Larsen (eds) *Central Places in the Migration and Merovingian Periods*, 317–331 (Uppsala: Almqvist and Wiksell International)

Suffolk County Council Archaeological Service, 2015 — *Ipswich 1974–1990 Excavation Archive*, York: Archaeology Data Service. Available: https://doi.org/10.5284/1034376. Accessed 20 October 2020

Sykes, N., 2007 — *The Norman Conquest: A Zooarchaeological Perspective* (Oxford: Archaeopress)

Sykes, N., Ayton, G., Bowen, F., Karis, B., Baker, P., Carden, R.F., Dicken, C., Evans, J., Hoelzel, A.R., Higham, T., Jones, R., Lamb, A., Liddiard, R., Madgwick, R., Miller, H., Rainsford, C., Sawyer, P., Thomas, R., Ward, C. and Whorley, F., 2016	'Wild to domestic and back again: The dynamics of fallow deer management in medieval England,' *STAR: Science and Technology of Archaeological Research* 2 (1), 113–26	Wade, K., 2001	'Ipswich,' in P. Crabtree (ed.), *Medieval Archaeology: An encyclopedia*, 173–5 (New York: Garland)
		Wade, K., 2013	*The Chronological Framework*. Available: http://archaeologydataservice.ac.uk/archiveDS/archiveDownload?t=arch-1644-1/dissemination/pdf/Metadata/The_Chronological_Framework_by_Keith_Wade.pdf
		Wade, K., forthcoming	*Excavations in Ipswich 1974–1990*, East Anglian Archaeology
Sykes, N., Craig-Atkins, E., Jervis, B. and A. McClain, 2019	*Archaeologies of the Norman Conquest*, Paper presented at the 84th Annual Meeting of the Society for American Archaeology (tDAR id: 451288), (Albuquerque, New Mexico)	Wade, K., n.d.	*A history of archaeology in Ipswich and of its Anglo-Saxon origins*, The Ipswich Archaeological Trust. Available: https://ipswichat.org.uk/AboutUs/History.aspx. Accessed 29 October 2020
Tester, A., Anderson, S., Riddler, I. and Carr, R., 2014	*Brandon, Staunch Meadow, Suffolk: A High Status Middle Saxon Settlement on the Fen Edge*, East Anglian Archaeology 151, 296–312 (Bury St Edmunds: Suffolk County Council Archaeological Service)	West, B., 1989	'Birds and mammals from the Peabody Site and National Gallery,' in R.L. Whitehead and R. Cowie, 'Excavations at the Peabody Site, Chandos Place, and the National Gallery,' *Transactions of the London and Middlesex Archaeological Society* 40, 150–168
		West, S.E., 1963	'Excavations at Cox Lane (1958) and the town defences, Shire Hall Yard (1959)' *Proceedings of the Suffolk Institute of Archaeology* 29, 233–303
The Landscape Partnership, 2012	*Quality Control: Heathland Restoration in the Suffolk Sandlings, Environmental Statement*		
Ulmschneider, K., 2000	'Settlement, economy and the 'productive' site: Middle Anglo-Saxon Lincolnshire, AD 650–780,' *Medieval Archaeology* 54, 53–77	Wutke S., Benecke N., Sandoval-Castellanos E., Döhle H.J., Friederich S., Gonzales J., Hallsteinn Hallsson J., Hofreiter M., Lõugas L., Magnell O., Morales-Muniz A., Orlando L., Pálsdóttir A.H., Reissmann M., Ruttkay M., Trinks A. and Ludwig A., 2016	'Spotted phenotypes in horses lost attractiveness in the Middle Ages,' *Scientific Reports*. DOI:10.1038/srep38548
Vince, A., 1984	'The Aldwych: Mid-Saxon London Discovered,' *Current Archaeology* 8 (4), 310–312		
Vince, A., 1990	*Saxon London: An Archaeological Investigation* (London: Seaby)		
von den Driesch, A., 1976	*A Guide to the Measurement of Animal Bones from Archaeological Sites*, Peabody Museum Bulletin 1 (Cambridge, Massachusetts: Peabody Museum of Archaeology and Ethnology, Harvard University)		
von den Driesch, A. and Boessneck, J., 1974	'Kritische Anmerkungen zur Widerristhohen berechnung aus Langenmasses vor- und frühgeschichtlicher Tierknocken,' *Saugetierkundliche Mitteilungen* 22, 325–348	Yalden, D. with Albarella, U., 2008	*The History of British Birds* (Oxford: Oxford University Press)
Wade, K., 1980	'A settlement at Bonhunt farm, Wicken Bonhunt, Essex,' in D.G. Buckley (ed.) *Archaeology in Essex to AD 1500*, Coun. Brit. Archaeol. Res. Rep. 34, 96–102 (London: Council for British Archaeology)	Zeder, M., 1988	'Understanding urban process through the study of specialized subsistence economy in the Near East,' *Journal of Anthropological Archaeology* 7, 1–55
Wade, K. 1988a	'Anglo-Saxon and Medieval Ipswich,' in Dymond, D. and Martin, E. (eds), *An Historical Atlas of Suffolk*, 122–123 (Ipswich: Suffolk County Council Planning Department and Suffolk Institute of Archaeology)	Zeder, M., 1991	*Feeding Cities: Specialized Animal Economy in the Ancient Near East* (Washington, DC: Smithsonian Institution Press)
		Zeder, M. and Lapham, H.A., 2010	'Assessing the reliability of criteria used to identify postcranial bones in sheep, *Ovis*, and goats, *Capra*,' *Journal of Archaeological Science* 37, 2887–2905
Wade, K., 1988b	'Ipswich,' in Hodges, R. and Hobley, B. (eds), *The Rebirth of Towns in the West, AD 700–1050*, Counc. Brit. Archaeol. Res. Rep. 68, 93–100 (London: Council for British Archaeology)	Zeder, M. and Pilaar, S., 2010	'Assessing the reliability of criteria used to identify mandibles and mandibular teeth in sheep, *Ovis*, and goats, *Capra*,' *Journal of Archaeological Science* 37, 225–242
Wade, K., 1993	'The urbanisation of East Anglia: the Ipswich Perspective,' in Julie Gardiner (ed.), *Flatlands and Wetlands: Current Themes in East Anglian Archaeology*, East Anglian Archaeology 50, 144–151		

Index

Page numbers in *italics* denote illustrations. Locations are in Ipswich unless indicated otherwise.

age profiles
   cattle
      Middle Saxon 14–15, *14*, 16
      Early Late Saxon 26, *27*, 28
      Middle Late Saxon 36, *36*, 37
      Early Medieval 43, *44*, 45
   pig
      Middle Saxon 16, 17, *19*
      Early Late Saxon 28, *29*
      Middle Late Saxon *36*, 37
      Early Medieval *44*, 45
   sheep/goat
      Middle Saxon 19–20, *20*
      Early Late Saxon 29–31, *30*
      Middle Late Saxon 38, 39, *39*
      Early Medieval 45, 46, *46*, *47*
amphibians 41, 55
antler-working 3, 25, 49
Antwerp (Belgium)
   assemblage 8
   hunting 12
   pigs 26, 50
   species ratios 11–12, *13*, 35
Arcade Street site (1804) 3, *4*
assemblages *see* faunal assemblages

Bayeux Tapestry 51
Bede 2, 8
birds
   discussion 51–2
   Middle Saxon 9, 13
   Early Late Saxon 25, 32
   Middle Late Saxon 34, 39
   Early Medieval 42, 47, *48*
body-part distributions
   Middle Saxon 13–14
   Early Late Saxon 25, 26
   Middle Late Saxon 35, 36
   Early Medieval 42, 43
bone-working 3, 25, 49
Bramwell, Don 5
Brandon (Suffolk)
   assemblage 7
   birds 9, 13, 21, 51
   dogs 31
   marine mammals 24
   pigs 16, 37
   sheep/goat 5, 17, 29, 38–9, 47
   species ratios 28, 50
Bridge Street site (6202) 3, *4*, 41, 54, 55
butchery
   horse 20–1, 31, 49, 51
   recording 5
Buttermarket 1–2
Buttermarket/St Stephen's Lane site (3104) 3, *4*, 41

Campana, Douglas 5
cattle
   discussion 49–50, *50*, 52, 53
   Middle Saxon 13–16, *16*, 17, *18*
   Early Late Saxon *18*, 25–6, *27*, 28
   Middle Late Saxon *18*, 36–7, *36*
   Early Medieval *18*, 43, *43*, *44*, 45
chicken
   discussion 51–52
   Middle Saxon 8, 13, 21, *21*
   Early Late Saxon 25, 32
   Middle Late Saxon 34, 39
   Early Medieval 42, 47, 48
cormorant 43
Corn Hill 2
corvids 49
   Middle Saxon 9, 13
   Early Late Saxon 25
   Middle Late Saxon 34
   Early Medieval 43
Cox Lane 1
Coy, Jennie 5
cranes 13, 25

dogs
   discussion 51
   Middle Saxon 8
   Early Late Saxon 31–2
   Middle Late Saxon 39
   Early Medieval 47
Dorestad (Neths)
   assemblage 7, 8
   cattle 15
   role of 2
   sheep/goat 17
   species ratios 11, 12, 13
ducks 25, 42

Early Late Saxon assemblages 23
   composition 23–5, *24*
   domestic birds 32
   domestic mammals 25–32
   provisioning Ipswich 32
Early Medieval assemblages 41
   composition 41–3
   domestic birds 47, *48*
   domestic mammals 43–7
   provisioning Ipswich 48
egg production 47, 48, 52
Elm Street 1
emporia 2
   archaeology of 7–8
   provisioning 52, 53
   species ratios 9–10, 11, *11*, 12, 13, *13*
excavations 1
   Early Middle Saxon (*c.* AD 600–700) 1–2
   Middle Saxon (AD 700–850/880) 2
   Early Late Saxon (*c.* AD 850/880–900) 2
   Middle Late Saxon (*c.* AD 900–1000) 2–3
   Early Medieval (*c.* AD 1000–1150) 3

falcons/falconry 25, 32, 34
fallow deer 25, 41
faunal assemblages, sources 3–5, *4*; *see also* Early Late Saxon assemblages; Early Medieval assemblages; Middle Late Saxon assemblages; Middle Saxon assemblages
Flixborough (Lincs) 24
Fore Street site (5902) 3, *4*
Foundation Street/School Lane site (4801) 3, *4*
Foundation Street/Star Lane site (5801) 3, *4*
Foundation Street/Wingfield Street site (4601) 3, *4*, 54, 55
fowling 13, 41, 49
fox 25, 41
future research 52–3

geese, domestic
   discussion 51–2
   Middle Saxon 9, 13
   Early Late Saxon 25
   Middle Late Saxon 34, 39
   Early Medieval 42, 47
Great Whip Street 1

Haithabu/Hedeby (Germany)
   assemblage 8
   cattle 15
   hunting/fowling 49
   sheep/goat 19
   species ratios 11, 12, 13

Hamwic (Hants)
    assemblage 7, 8
    cattle 15, 22
    horse 21
    hunting/fowling 13
    occupation 23
    pigs 16, 37
    provisioning 22, 52
    sheep/goat 5, 17–19, 20, 38
    species ratios 9–10, 11, *11*, 35
hares 34, 41
hawks/hawking 25, 32, 43
horn-working 3, 5, 17
horse
    discussion 49, 51
    Middle Saxon 8, 9–10, *10*, 14, 20–1
    Early Late Saxon 24, 25, 26, 31
    Middle Late Saxon 34, *34*, 35, 39
    Early Medieval *42*, 43, 47
hunting
    discussion 49
    evidence
        Middle Saxon 9, 12, 13
        Early Late Saxon 25, 32
        Early Medieval 41
    research questions 5
Hurst, John 1

Icklingham (Suffolk) 38

Jones, Roger 5

Key Street site (5901) 3, *4*

Late Saxon *see* Early Late Saxon; Middle Late Saxon
Lincoln (Lincs), Flaxengate 34, 35
Little Whip Street site (7404) 3, *4*
Lower Brook Street 1
Lundenwic
    assemblage 8
    cattle 15
    decline 23
    hunting/fowling 12, 13
    sheep/goat 15, 20
    species ratios 9–10, 11, *11*, 12, 13

Maltby, Mark 5
markets 22, 32, 52
meat supply 52
    Middle Saxon 21–2
    Early Late Saxon 32
    Middle Late Saxon 40
    Early Medieval 48
Middle Late Saxon assemblages 33–4
    composition 34–5, *34*
    domestic birds 39
    domestic mammals 35–9
    provisioning Ipswich 40
Middle Saxon assemblages
    composition 8–13, *10*, *11*, *13*
    domestic birds 21, *21*
    domestic mammals 13–21
    emporium sites and roles of 7–8
    provisioning Ipswich 21–2

Norwich (Norfolk) 35

Origins of Ipswich Project 1, 8

peregrine falcon 34
pig
    discussion 50, *51*, 52, 53
    Middle Saxon 9–12, *10*, *13*, 14, 16–17, 19, *19*
    Early Late Saxon 24, 25, 26–8, *28*, *29*
    Middle Late Saxon 34–5, *34*, *36*, 37, 38
    Early Medieval *42*, 43, 45
pigeons 25, 42
Pirenne, Henri 7

Quentovic (France) 2, 8, 11, 12, 13

rabbits 34, 41
red deer 49
    Middle Saxon 9, 12
    Early Late Saxon 25
    Middle Late Saxon 34
    Early Medieval 41
Rendlesham (Suffolk) 2
research questions 5
Ribe (Denmark)
    assemblage 8
    cattle 11
    horse 21
    hunting/fowling 12, 13, 49
    sheep/goat 19, 20
roe deer 49
    Middle Saxon 9, 12
    Early Late Saxon 25
    Middle Late Saxon 34
    Early Medieval 41

St Albans (Herts) 11
St George's Street site (9802) 3, *4*, 55
St Nicholas Street site (4201) 3, *4*, 25, 49
St Peter's Street site (5203) 3, *4*, 5, 8–9, 39, 54
Sandlings (Suffolk) 35, 50, 52
sheep/goat
    discussion 50–1, 52, 53
    identification 5
    Middle Saxon 9–10, *10*, 11, *13*, 14, 17–20, *20*
    Early Late Saxon 24, 25, 26, 28, 29–31, *30*, 32
    Middle Late Saxon 34, *34*, 35, 38–9, *39*
    Early Medieval *42*, 43, 45–7, *47*, 48
Shire Hall 1
Shire Hall Yard site (6904) 3, *4*, 34
size
    cattle
        Middle Saxon 15–16, *16*
        Early Late Saxon 25–6, *27*
        Middle Late Saxon 36–7
        Early Medieval *43*, 44
    dog 31–2
    horse 21, 31
    pig
        Middle Saxon 16–17, 19
        Early Late Saxon 28
        Middle Late Saxon 37, 38
        Early Medieval 45
    sheep/goat
        Middle Saxon 17–19
        Early Late Saxon 29, *30*, 32
        Middle Late Saxon 38–9
        Early Medieval 46, 47
species ratios
    discussion 49, *49*
    Middle Saxon 9–12, *10*, *11*, *13*
    Early Late Saxon 24, *24*, 25, 32
    Middle Late Saxon 34–5, *34*
    Early Medieval *42*, 43
Stevens, Patricia 5
Stoke Quay 2
Suffolk County Archaeological Unit 1
Sutton Hoo (Suffolk) 2

Tacket Street site (3410) 3, *4*, 34
teal 42
Thetford (Norfolk) 32, 34, 35
Tower Ramparts site (0802) 3, *4*, 54, 55
trade 2, 3, 7–8
Tranmer House (Suffolk) 2
Turrett Lane 1

urban provisioning 52; *see also* meat supply

Vernon Street 1
Viking control 2, 23, 32

Wade, Keith 1
West, Stanley 1
West Stow (Suffolk)
    birds 9, 13

cattle 15–16, *16*
dog 31
sheep/goat
  age 29–31, *30*, 47
  distinguishing 5
  size 17, 29, 32, 38, 50
  species ratios 28
West Stow West (Suffolk) 13, 28
whale 24, 32, 41
Wicken Bonhunt (Essex) 7, 11, 12, 13, 37, 51
wics see emporia
William I 3
Winchester (Hants)
  assemblage 33–4
  birds 39, 52
  cattle 36, 50
  dogs 32
  horse 39
  pigs 35
  sheep/goat 38
  species ratios 35

York (Yorks)
  assemblage 8, 23, 25, 33
  cattle 15, 16
  dogs 32
  horse 51
  hunting/fowling 12, 13
  marine mammals 24
  sheep/goat 20, 47
  species ratios 9–10, 11, *11*, 12, 13, 35+

East Anglian Archaeology
is a serial publication sponsored by ALGAO EE and English Heritage. It is the main vehicle for publishing final reports on archaeological excavations and surveys in the region. For information about titles in the series, visit **http://eaareports.org.uk**. Reports can be obtained from:
Oxbow Books, **https://www.oxbowbooks.com/oxbow/eaa**
or directly from the organisation publishing a particular volume.

Reports available so far:

No.1,	1975	Suffolk: various papers
No.2,	1976	Norfolk: various papers
No.3,	1977	Suffolk: various papers
No.4,	1976	Norfolk: Late Saxon town of Thetford
No.5,	1977	Norfolk: various papers on Roman sites
No.6,	1977	Norfolk: Spong Hill Anglo-Saxon cemetery, Part I
No.7,	1978	Norfolk: Bergh Apton Anglo-Saxon cemetery
No.8,	1978	Norfolk: various papers
No.9,	1980	Norfolk: North Elmham Park
No.10,	1980	Norfolk: village sites in Launditch Hundred
No.11,	1981	Norfolk: Spong Hill, Part II: Catalogue of Cremations
No.12,	1981	The barrows of East Anglia
No.13,	1981	Norwich: Eighteen centuries of pottery from Norwich
No.14,	1982	Norfolk: various papers
No.15,	1982	Norwich: Excavations in Norwich 1971–1978; Part I
No.16,	1982	Norfolk: Beaker domestic sites in the Fen-edge and East Anglia
No.17,	1983	Norfolk: Waterfront excavations and Thetford-type Ware production, Norwich
No.18,	1983	Norfolk: The archaeology of Witton
No.19,	1983	Norfolk: Two post-medieval earthenware pottery groups from Fulmodeston
No.20,	1983	Norfolk: Burgh Castle: excavation by Charles Green, 1958–61
No.21,	1984	Norfolk: Spong Hill, Part III: Catalogue of Inhumations
No.22,	1984	Norfolk: Excavations in Thetford, 1948–59 and 1973–80
No.23,	1985	Norfolk: Excavations at Brancaster 1974 and 1977
No.24,	1985	Suffolk: West Stow, the Anglo-Saxon village
No.25,	1985	Essex: Excavations by Mr H.P.Cooper on the Roman site at Hill Farm, Gestingthorpe, Essex
No.26,	1985	Norwich: Excavations in Norwich 1971–78; Part II
No.27,	1985	Cambridgeshire: The Fenland Project No.1: Archaeology and Environment in the Lower Welland Valley
No.28,	1985	Norfolk: Excavations within the north-east bailey of Norwich Castle, 1978
No.29,	1986	Norfolk: Barrow excavations in Norfolk, 1950–82
No.30,	1986	Norfolk: Excavations at Thornham, Warham, Wighton and Caistor St Edmund, Norfolk
No.31,	1986	Norfolk: Settlement, religion and industry on the Fen-edge; three Romano-British sites in Norfolk
No.32,	1987	Norfolk: Three Norman Churches in Norfolk
No.33,	1987	Essex: Excavation of a Cropmark Enclosure Complex at Woodham Walter, Essex, 1976 and An Assessment of Excavated Enclosures in Essex
No.34,	1987	Norfolk: Spong Hill, Part IV: Catalogue of Cremations
No.35,	1987	Cambridgeshire: The Fenland Project No.2: Fenland Landscapes and Settlement, Peterborough–March
No.36,	1987	Norfolk: The Anglo-Saxon Cemetery at Morningthorpe
No.37,	1987	Norfolk: Excavations at St Martin-at-Palace Plain, Norwich, 1981
No.38,	1988	Suffolk: The Anglo-Saxon Cemetery at Westgarth Gardens, Bury St Edmunds
No.39,	1988	Norfolk: Spong Hill, Part VI: Occupation during the 7th–2nd millennia BC
No.40,	1988	Suffolk: Burgh: The Iron Age and Roman Enclosure
No.41,	1988	Essex: Excavations at Great Dunmow, Essex: a Romano-British small town in the Trinovantian Civitas
No.42,	1988	Essex: Archaeology and Environment in South Essex, Rescue Archaeology along the Gray's By-pass 1979–80
No.43,	1988	Essex: Excavation at the North Ring, Mucking, Essex: A Late Bronze Age Enclosure
No.44,	1988	Norfolk: Six Deserted Villages in Norfolk
No.45,	1988	Norfolk: The Fenland Project No. 3: Marshland and the Nar Valley, Norfolk
No.46,	1989	Norfolk: The Deserted Medieval Village of Thuxton
No.47,	1989	Suffolk: West Stow: Early Anglo-Saxon Animal Husbandry
No.48,	1989	Suffolk: West Stow, Suffolk: The Prehistoric and Romano-British Occupations
No.49,	1990	Norfolk: The Evolution of Settlement in Three Parishes in South-East Norfolk
No.50,	1993	Proceedings of the Flatlands and Wetlands Conference
No.51,	1991	Norfolk: The Ruined and Disused Churches of Norfolk
No.52,	1991	Norfolk: The Fenland Project No. 4, The Wissey Embayment and Fen Causeway
No.53,	1992	Norfolk: Excavations in Thetford, 1980–82, Fison Way
No.54,	1992	Norfolk: The Iron Age Forts of Norfolk
No.55,	1992	Lincolnshire: The Fenland Project No.5: Lincolnshire Survey, The South-West Fens
No.56,	1992	Cambridgeshire: The Fenland Project No.6: The South-Western Cambridgeshire Fens
No.57,	1993	Norfolk and Lincolnshire: Excavations at Redgate Hill Hunstanton; and Tattershall Thorpe
No.58,	1993	Norwich: Households: The Medieval and Post-Medieval Finds from Norwich Survey Excavations 1971–1978
No.59,	1993	Fenland: The South-West Fen Dyke Survey Project 1982–86
No.60,	1993	Norfolk: Caister-on-Sea: Excavations by Charles Green, 1951–55
No.61,	1993	Fenland: The Fenland Project No.7: Excavations in Peterborough and the Lower Welland Valley 1960–1969
No.62,	1993	Norfolk: Excavations in Thetford by B.K. Davison, between 1964 and 1970
No.63,	1993	Norfolk: Illington: A Study of a Breckland Parish and its Anglo-Saxon Cemetery
No.64,	1994	Norfolk: The Late Saxon and Medieval Pottery Industry of Grimston: Excavations 1962–92
No.65,	1993	Suffolk: Settlements on Hill-tops: Seven Prehistoric Sites in Suffolk
No.66,	1993	Lincolnshire: The Fenland Project No.8: Lincolnshire Survey, the Northern Fen-Edge
No.67,	1994	Norfolk: Spong Hill, Part V: Catalogue of Cremations
No.68,	1994	Norfolk: Excavations at Fishergate, Norwich 1985
No.69,	1994	Norfolk: Spong Hill, Part VIII: The Cremations
No.70,	1994	Fenland: The Fenland Project No.9: Flandrian Environmental Change in Fenland
No.71,	1995	Essex: The Archaeology of the Essex Coast Vol.I: The Hullbridge Survey Project
No.72,	1995	Norfolk: Excavations at Redcastle Furze, Thetford, 1988–9
No.73,	1995	Norfolk: Spong Hill, Part VII: Iron Age, Roman and Early Saxon Settlement
No.74,	1995	Norfolk: A Late Neolithic, Saxon and Medieval Site at Middle Harling
No.75,	1995	Essex: North Shoebury: Settlement and Economy in South-east Essex 1500–AD1500
No.76,	1996	Nene Valley: Orton Hall Farm: A Roman and Early Anglo-Saxon Farmstead
No.77,	1996	Norfolk: Barrow Excavations in Norfolk, 1984–88
No.78,	1996	Norfolk:The Fenland Project No.11: The Wissey Embayment: Evidence for pre-Iron Age Occupation
No.79,	1996	Cambridgeshire: The Fenland Project No.10: Cambridgeshire Survey, the Isle of Ely and Wisbech
No.80,	1997	Norfolk: Barton Bendish and Caldecote: fieldwork in south-west Norfolk
No.81,	1997	Norfolk: Castle Rising Castle
No.82,	1998	Essex: Archaeology and the Landscape in the Lower Blackwater Valley
No.83,	1998	Essex: Excavations south of Chignall Roman Villa 1977–81
No.84,	1998	Suffolk: A Corpus of Anglo-Saxon Material
No.85,	1998	Suffolk: Towards a Landscape History of Walsham le Willows
No.86,	1998	Essex: Excavations at the Orsett 'Cock' Enclosure
No.87,	1999	Norfolk: Excavations in Thetford, North of the River, 1989–90
No.88,	1999	Essex: Excavations at Ivy Chimneys, Witham 1978–83
No.89,	1999	Lincolnshire: Salterns: Excavations at Helpringham, Holbeach St Johns and Bicker Haven
No.90,	1999	Essex:The Archaeology of Ardleigh, Excavations 1955–80
No.91,	2000	Norfolk: Excavations on the Norwich Southern Bypass, 1989–91 Part I Bixley, Caistor St Edmund, Trowse
No.92,	2000	Norfolk: Excavations on the Norwich Southern Bypass, 1989–91 Part II Harford Farm Anglo-Saxon Cemetery
No.93,	2001	Norfolk: Excavations on the Snettisham Bypass, 1989
No.94,	2001	Lincolnshire: Excavations at Billingborough, 1975–8
No.95,	2001	Suffolk: Snape Anglo-Saxon Cemetery: Excavations and Surveys
No.96,	2001	Norfolk: Two Medieval Churches in Norfolk
No.97,	2001	Nene Valley: Monument 97, Orton Longueville

No.98,	2002	Essex: Excavations at Little Oakley, 1951–78
No.99,	2002	Norfolk: Excavations at Melford Meadows, Brettenham, 1994
No.100,	2002	Norwich: Excavations in Norwich 1971–78, Part III
No.101,	2002	Norfolk: Medieval Armorial Horse Furniture in Norfolk
No.102,	2002	Norfolk: Baconsthorpe Castle, Excavations and Finds, 1951–1972
No.103,	2003	Cambridgeshire: Excavations at the Wardy Hill Ringwork, Coveney, Ely
No.104,	2003	Norfolk: Earthworks of Norfolk
No.105	2003	Essex: Excavations at Great Holts Farm, 1992–4
No.106	2004	Suffolk: Romano-British Settlement at Hacheston
No.107	2004	Essex: Excavations at Stansted Airport, 1986–91
No.108,	2004	Norfolk: Excavations at Mill Lane, Thetford, 1995
No.109,	2005	Fenland: Archaeology and Environment of the Etton Landscape
No.110,	2005	Cambridgeshire: Saxon and Medieval Settlement at West Fen Road, Ely
No.111,	2005	Essex: Early Anglo-Saxon Cemetery and Later Saxon Settlement at Springfield Lyons
No.112,	2005	Norfolk: Dragon Hall, King Street, Norwich
No.113,	2006	Norfolk: Excavations at Kilverstone
No.114,	2006	Cambridgeshire:Waterfront Archaeology in Ely
No.115,	2006	Essex:Medieval Moated Manor by the Thames Estuary: Excavations at Southchurch Hall, Southend
No.116,	2006	Norfolk: Norwich Cathedral Refectory
No.117,	2007	Essex: Excavations at Lodge Farm, St Osyth
No.118,	2007	Essex: Late Iron Age Warrior Burial from Kelvedon
No.119,	2007	Norfolk: Aspects of Anglo-Saxon Inhumation Burial
No.120,	2007	Norfolk: Norwich Greyfriars: Pre-Conquest Town and Medieval Friary
No.121,	2007	Cambridgeshire: A Line Across Land: Fieldwork on the Isleham–Ely Pipeline 1993–4
No.122,	2008	Cambridgeshire: Ely Wares
No.123,	2008	Cambridgeshire: Farming on the Edge: Archaeological Evidence from the Clay Uplands west of Cambridge
No.124,	2008	*Wheare most Inclosures be*, East Anglian Fields: History, Morphology and Management
No.125,	2008	Bedfordshire: Life in the Loop: a Prehistoric and Romano-British Landscape at Biddenham
No.126,	2008	Essex: Early Neolithic Ring-ditch and Bronze Age Cemetery at Brightlingsea
No.127,	2008	Essex: Early Saxon Cemetery at Rayleigh
No.128,	2009	Hertfordshire: Four Millennia of Human Activity along the A505 Baldock Bypass
No.129,	2009	Norfolk: Criminals and Paupers: the Graveyard of St Margaret Fyebriggate *in combusto*, Norwich
No.130,	2009	Norfolk: A Medieval Cemetery at Mill Lane, Ormesby St Margaret
No.131,	2009	Suffolk: Anglo-Saxon Settlement and Cemetery at Bloodmoor Hill, Carlton Colville
No.132,	2009	Norfolk: Norwich Castle: Excavations and Historical Survey 1987–98 (Parts I–IV)
No.133,	2010	Norfolk: Life and Death on a Norwich Backstreet, AD900–1600: Excavations in St Faith's Lane
No.134,	2010	Norfolk: Farmers and Ironsmiths: Prehistoric, Roman and Anglo-Saxon Settlement beside Brandon Road, Thetford
No.135,	2011	Norfolk: Romano-British and Saxon Occupation at Billingford
No.136,	2011	Essex: Aerial Archaeology in Essex
No.137,	2011	Essex: The Roman Town of Great Chesterford
No.138,	2011	Bedfordshire: Farm and Forge: late Iron Age/Romano-British farmsteads at Marsh Leys, Kempston
No.139,	2011	Suffolk: The Anglo-Saxon Cemetery at Shrubland Hall Quarry, Coddenham
No.140,	2011	Norfolk: Archaeology of the Newland: Excavations in King's Lynn, 2003–5
No.141,	2011	Cambridgeshire: Life and Afterlife at Duxford: archaeology and history in a chalkland community
No.142,	2012	Cambridgeshire: *Extraordinary Inundations of the Sea*: Excavations at Market Mews, Wisbech
No.143,	2012	Middle Saxon Animal Husbandry in East Anglia
No.144,	2012	Essex: The Archaeology of the Essex Coast Vol.II: Excavations at the Prehistoric Site of the Stumble
No.145,	2012	Norfolk: Bacton to King's Lynn Gas Pipeline Vol.1: Prehistoric, Roman and Medieval Archaeology
No.146,	2012	Suffolk: Experimental Archaeology and Fire: a Burnt Reconstruction at West Stow Anglo-Saxon Village
No.147,	2012	Suffolk: Circles and Cemeteries: Excavations at Flixton Vol. I
No.148,	2012	Essex: Hedingham Ware: a medieval pottery industry in North Essex; its production and distribution
No.149,	2013	Essex: The Neolithic and Bronze Age Enclosures at Springfield Lyons
No.150,	2013	Norfolk: Tyttel's *Halh*: the Anglo-Saxon Cemetery at Tittleshall. The Archaeology of the Bacton to King's Lynn Gas Pipeline Vol.2
No.151,	2014	Suffolk: Staunch Meadow, Brandon: a High Status Middle Saxon Settlement on the Fen Edge
No.152,	2014	A Romano-British Settlement in the Waveney Valley: Excavations at Scole 1993–4
No.153,	2015	Peterborough: A Late Saxon Village and Medieval Manor: Excavations at Botolph Bridge, Orton Longueville
No.154,	2015	Essex: Heybridge, a Late Iron Age and Roman Settlement: Excavations at Elms Farm 1993–5 Vol. 1
No.155,	2015	Suffolk: Before Sutton Hoo: the prehistoric remains and Early Anglo-Saxon cemetery at Tranmer House, Bromeswell
No.156,	2016	Bedfordshire: Close to the Loop: landscape and settlement evolution beside the Biddenham Loop, west of Bedford
No.157,	2016	Cambridgeshire: Bronze Age Barrow, Early to Middle Iron Age Settlement and Burials, Early Anglo-Saxon Settlement at Harston Mill
No.158,	2016	Bedfordshire: Newnham: a Roman bath house and estate centre east of Bedford
No.159,	2016	Cambridgeshire: The Production and Distribution of Medieval Pottery in Cambridgeshire
No.160,	2016	Suffolk: A Late Iron-Age and Romano-British Farmstead at Cedars Park, Stowmarket
No.161,	2016	Suffolk: Medieval Dispersed Settlement on the Mid Suffolk Clay at Cedars Park, Stowmarket
No.162,	2017	Cambridgeshire: The Horningsea Roman Pottery Industry in Context
No.163,	2018	Nene Valley: Iron Age and Roman Settlement: Rescue Excavations at Lynch Farm 2, Orton Longueville, Peterborough
No.164,	2018	Suffolk: Excavations at Wixoe Roman Small Town
No.165,	2018	Cambridgeshire: Conquering the Claylands: Excavations at Love's Farm, St Neots
No.166,	2018	Norfolk: Late Bronze Age Hoards: new light on old finds
No.167,	2018	Norfolk: A Romano-British Industrial Site at East Winch
No.168,	2018	Cambridgeshire: Small Communities: Life in the Cam Valley in the Neolithic, Late Iron Age and Early Anglo-Saxon Periods. Excavations at Dernford Farm, Sawston
No.169,	2019	Suffolk: Iron Age Fortification Beside the River Lark: Excavations at Mildenhall
No.170,	2019	Cambridgeshire: Rectory Farm, Godmanchester: Excavations 1988–95, Neolithic monument to Roman villa farm
No.171,	2020	Norfolk: Three Bronze Age Weapon Assemblages
No.172,	2020	Suffolk: Excavations at Stoke Quay, Ipswich: Southern *Gipeswic* and the parish of St Augustine
No.173,	2020	Nene Valley:Prehistoric Burial Mounds in Orton Meadows, Peterborough
No.174,	2021	Suffolk: Provisioning Ipswich: Animal Remains from the Saxon and Medieval Town